CLASS STRATIFICATION

A Comparative Perspective

Richard Breen

David B. Rottman

HARVESTER
WHEATSHEAF

New York   London   Toronto   Sydney   Tokyo   Singapore

First published 1995 by
Harvester Wheatsheaf
Campus 400, Maylands Avenue
Hemel Hempstead
Hertfordshire, HP2 7EZ
A division of
Simon & Schuster International Group

Typeset in 10/12pt Times
by Photoprint, Torquay, S. Devon

Printed and bound in Great Britain by
Hartnolls Ltd, Bodmin, Cornwall

Library of Congress Cataloging-in-Publication Data

Breen, Richard, 1954–
    Class stratification: a comparative perspective / Richard Breen
and David B. Rottman.
        p.   cm.
    Includes bibliographical references and index.
    ISBN 0–7450–1268–X
    1. Social classes.   I. Rottman, David B.   II. Title.
HT609.B74   1995
305.5—dc20
                                                        94–29721
                                                        CIP

British Library Cataloguing in Publication Data

A catalogue record for this book is available from the British
Library

ISBN: 0 7450 1268 X

---

   2   3   4   5   99   98   97

CONTENTS

WHAT THIS BOOK IS ABOUT

In this book we develop a new approach to the sociological study of stratification. The novelty arises primarily because our starting point is the behaviour of individuals and secondarily because the scope of our presentation is broadly international. These claims call for some preliminary words to explain why we believe that the result is an enhanced understanding of social stratification.

The need for elaboration and justification is strongest for the attention we place on the behaviour of individuals. Stratification is concerned with groups, and it may seem – indeed is – an unusual step to devote the initial chapter of our book to the behaviour of individuals. Now groups, of course, consist of individuals, and it is common to assert that all social phenomena must ultimately be understood as the product of the actions and interaction of individuals (e.g. Elster 1989:13). What is rare is for the micro-sociological foundations of stratification theory to be so clearly detailed and then used to explain why persons in a group share a number of attributes including similar chances for material success. Briefly, the essence of stratification is that individuals are unequally located within a structure of social power. By social power we mean the set of resources individuals possess to enable them to pursue certain sorts of actions and the constraints they face in doing so. Social stratification in our approach seeks to explain the bases through which individuals come to share particular positions of social power. In advanced societies, those bases include gender, ethnicity, and class. Our focus is on class, the position of social power that derives from location in the production process. Class is the most important determinant of life chances because it directly links individuals to the economic order.

The payoff from explaining all of this at the outset is a clearer picture of what a class is and why class is so important. We hope that, as a result, readers will be able to understand how the often nebulous concept of class affects their lives. This contrasts with accounts of class that begin at the group level and thus leave unanswered the question of why being a member of a social class has particular consequences. Students of stratification often sound almost apologetic for persisting in emphasizing the idea of 'social class' in an era where the term has largely slipped out of everyday usage. This is unnecessary. Contemporary theories can often be uncertain guides as to where we should expect class to matter precisely because they lack a grounding in individual behaviour.

One upshot of laying a solid foundation in the behaviour of individuals is a rigorous and transparent definition of class stratification for use when describing and analyzing the class structure of nations. This leads to the second novel feature of the book. We adopt an explicitly comparative perspective. The potential of the study of social stratification, and particularly class stratification, is most importantly realized in what it can tell us about similarities and differences among nations. Fundamentally, nations differ in the bases of social power around which groups are likely to form. The understanding that we have of how the behaviour of individuals is linked to class position offers insight into the divergent patterns of openness or closure observed in various countries and the degrees of distributional conflict present.

We proceed to examine some of the main points of similarity and difference among the advanced industrial societies. To do so, we draw upon the considerable body of comparable data on national class structures and patterns of social mobility.

To describe and compare class structures requires theories that tell us how social classes are defined and the procedures for allocating people to classes. With Chapter 1 stating our approach to understanding how social class relates to individual behaviour, our second chapter begins with a concise overview of the classical ideas of Karl Marx and Max Weber, but concentrates on the major strands within contemporary class theory. Chapter 3 takes up the ideas of two prominent contemporary class theorists and explains how each moves from their theoretical concepts to specific instructions for placing individuals into class positions.

Class is a central theoretical concept in sociology. Chapters 4, 5, and 6 put the utility of the concept to the test. The national class structures of several European and non-European countries are compared in Chapter 4 and the macro-sociological factors currently reshaping those class structures are outlined. Chapter 5 turns to the study of social mobility, a key indicator of societal openness and of the strength of class boundaries. Patterns of movement by individuals and families between places in the class structures of several countries are analyzed. Chapter 6 looks at class in geographical perspective by considering the extent to which a nation's position within the world economy and political order has implications for the class structure that prevails. In short, what is the relationship between class stratification within a nation and that nation's place in the world order?

The theoretical and empirical status of class is currently under challenge. In Chapter 7 we consider these critiques of class analysis and assess the merits of claims being made for the primacy of alternative bases of stratification such as race.

The concluding chapter is concerned more with looking forward than with reviewing what has already been presented and debated. As is standard in concluding chapters, we propose issues and problems, both theoretical and methodological, that merit attention. But we concentrate on the enduring relevance of class as an analytical tool for understanding contemporary societies, as well as the shape of our individual lives. The social class into which we are born remains vastly influential in shaping our life course and life chances, even in the waning years of the twentieth century.

CHAPTER 1

MAKING SENSE OF STRATIFICATION

Introduction

The term 'stratification' conjures up an image of the population divided into groups which are like strata, one placed above another (Worsley *et al.* 1977:395). Such an image is both striking and persuasive: yet incorporating the concept of stratification into the study of society brings with it numerous problems, both conceptual (how do we define a stratum?) and empirical (who should be assigned to which stratum and on what basis?). These difficulties, however, are not evident at first sight: the idea that society consists of groups, arranged hierarchically like rock strata or the steps of a pyramid or the tiers of a wedding cake is a common one.

It is precisely because developing a rigorous use of the term 'social stratification' is more awkward than it might appear that we devote this first chapter to basics: in particular we believe that it is important to ground the study of stratification in a model of individual social action. This is true notwithstanding the fact that, in the study of stratification, the focus is on groups in society (the strata) rather than individuals. All groups are made up of individuals and to explain the behaviour of groups and the relations between them requires that we show how these arise 'as the result of the action and interaction of individuals' (Elster 1989:13). Hence we begin with a model of the individual person (or 'actor') in society. What emerges is a view of stratification as the study of social power and its distribution. By social power we refer to the resources that an individual possesses that enable him or her to undertake actions, and to the constraints attached to alternative choices of action. The actions of concern to us are those that affect people's life chances, the ability to share in the good things in life, both economic and social.

A model of choices, preferences, constraints, and resources

An important part of social life consists of people making choices about which particular course of action they should pursue. Should I stay at school or leave? Should I take the job that has been offered to me or keep the job I have? Should I buy a carton of milk or a Danish pastry? In all these cases choices are made between alternatives, which can be ranked in order of preference: but the only relevant choices are those that are available to the actor. For example, the job I prefer over all others might be that of a professional tennis player, but unfortunately this alternative is not open to me: technically it does not fall into my choice set. The alternatives that do are those whose costs are within the capacity of my resources. Within the alternatives that meet this condition, the costs of each will probably differ. So, if I have a certain amount of money and I want to buy a new car, the only cars that I can possibly buy must not cost more than the amount of money I have, but, among the set of cars that meet this condition, prices will vary. In choosing between the available alternatives, I will try to make the best deal in the trade-off between how much each alternative costs and how strongly I prefer it.

This approach, which views actors as utilizing resources in order to make choices between differentially preferred alternatives each of which carries a cost, is widespread in the social sciences: indeed, economics is based on exactly this model. In economics costs are usually identified with prices, resources with what is called the individual's 'budget constraint', and preferences with the 'utility' attached by the individual to the different alternatives. Within the neo-classical microeconomic framework this provides the basis for a powerful model of individual economic behaviour, albeit one which rests on some equally strong and, many have argued, debatable assumptions about individual rationality and the nature of individual preferences. In sociology and some of the other social sciences this approach is most developed in 'rational choice' theory.[1] This is well summarized and illustrated in the collections edited by Elster (1986) and Coleman and Farraro (1992) and in some of the contributions in Swedberg (1990). Even when the rational choice approach is not explicitly invoked, the model we have outlined can be found at the basis of much sociological theorizing. For example, in his work on social mobility (which we will discuss in detail in Chapter 5) John Goldthorpe (1980/87:99) argues that patterns of mobility between social classes are shaped by three factors. These are the relative *desirability* of different classes as destinations (in other words, preferences); the *resources* available to individuals that will allow them access to more desirable classes; and *barriers to mobility* – which we conceptualize in terms of costs, or, more generally, as *constraints* on actions.

The pervasiveness of this simple idea can be seen in the breadth of topics to which it can be applied. One good example of this is the way the model can be applied to interaction between individuals. For example, consider a salesman and a woman who comes into a shop to buy a vacuum cleaner. The salesman may have had a late night, be suffering from a hangover, and have had an argument with his teenage son before he left the house that morning. His preference would be to tell the customer to go away and buy her vacuum cleaner somewhere else. What stops him telling her this and why, instead, does he act in a respectful and polite fashion towards her? The answer is obvious: if he told customers to go away and do their shopping somewhere else, he would soon lose his job. Besides, he also wants to make a sale to earn commission, and he knows that, to accomplish this, one thing he must do is behave in a polite and friendly manner towards the customer. Why? Because this is what he believes the customer expects. In this situation, then, there are several alternatives that the salesman could choose, all of which carry costs. Of them all, the one which is preferred (telling the customer to go away) is also the most costly, both in terms of the risk of losing his job and in terms of the commission he will certainly not get.

We all find ourselves, from time to time, in situations in which we know we should express some sort of deference or respect for the person with whom we are talking (or, more generally, interacting). Whether, in any given instance, we do behave in this way is up to us: but if we fail to behave in the 'appropriate' fashion, we will probably have to bear the cost.

The important issue, from the point of view of the study of social stratification, is not simply that actors make choices within this framework of resources, constraints, and preferences, but that different people have different resources and face different sets of constraints.[2] That different people have different resources is easily seen if we think of economic behaviour where resources can often be identified with the amount of money someone has. In addition, however, different people face different constraints on their actions. So, for example, the driver of a police car could go through a red light with impunity, while a customer who had a sufficiently large and important bank account could probably be quite rude to a bank manager and still get the loan he or she wanted, while someone with more modest financial assets probably could not.

The differential distribution of resources and constraints is extremely important in explaining differences in behaviour. People who possess similar resources and face similar sorts of costs attached to actions frequently behave in ways that are similar when making a particular choice, and differently from people who face different constraints and/or have different resources. So, in Northern Ireland (and in many other societies), a man or woman is much more likely to marry someone of his or her own religion (Catholic or Protestant in Northern Ireland) than someone from the other religious grouping. This is partly, but not entirely, because the constraints (such as the possible social ostracism from family and friends) on marrying someone of the other religion are so substantial. The result is that very few Protestants marry Catholics, and the majority of marriages are between people of the same religion.

This idea can be applied to what we might call 'strategic choices'. Individuals may overcome constraints by means of strategic action. So, an individual worker may be powerless to compel her employer to, say, improve her working conditions; but if she can organize her fellow workers in collective action (through forming a trade union, for example) then the employer may be forced to make some changes. Such strategic action itself, however, is hedged with constraints and people face different constraints in pursuing such action (for example, trade unions are illegal in some countries). Or consider the case of parliamentary lobbying. One function of this is to persuade legislators to amend the law in a way that favours the lobbyists. Obviously, not all individuals in society have the resources that would allow them to engage in this kind of activity. What is perhaps most interesting about this example, however, is that it demonstrates that some actors, through strategic action in one arena, can change the 'rules of the game' (the set of constraints acting upon the process of choice) in some other arena.

Social regularities

In many areas of social life, people make choices, in which they seek to acquire what they most prefer, subject to the constraints they face and the resources they possess. To the extent to which people have similar resources and face the same set of constraints (and have the same preferences) they largely make the same choices. So, undergraduates do not have to take their examinations – they are free to decline the offer. However, most of them do, and the consequences of not doing so are clear to all. There are two important, and related, points to make here. First, we should stress that we are talking about choices that people make – in other words, we accept that people have free will and that they are free to make up their own minds about what choices to make, what courses of action to pursue, and so on. But, where people are placed in much the same position with respect to resources and constraints, they will *tend* to make the same choices. The relation-ship between sharing the same position and making the same choices is probabilistic (rather than deterministic). That is to say, the greater the extent to which different people have the same resources and face the same set of constraints on their choices, the greater is the probability that their choices will be the same. Therefore, not all Catholics in Northern Ireland marry other Catholics – but the great majority do. Likewise, not all customers seeking a loan are polite to their bank manager – but most are. And not all sales people are friendly and polite to customers.

The second, and related, point, is that the result of this is the existence of what are called *aggregate regularities* in social life. Many of these are encapsulated in well-known social facts such as that children from working-class families are much more likely to leave school without qualifications than are children from middle-class backgrounds. Such regularities are striking because they are so strong, and yet they arise from the independent decisions made by individuals.

The important distinction here is between individual events (which are not predictable) and aggregate behaviour (which is much more predictable). This link can be illustrated using a simple analogy. A single throw of a dice is not predictable: there is (if the dice is unbiased) an equal chance of its coming down on any of its six sides. But the result of a large number of throws of the dice (or of a single throw of a large number of dice) is predictable: we know that the average of the rolls of the dice will be roughly three and a half.[3]

In fact, regularities underpin all of social interaction. A little thought will be sufficient to convince anyone that, if social life were not regular (and thus predictable – albeit in a probabilistic rather than deterministic sense), it would not be possible. Suppose, for example, that when I met people I had absolutely no idea how they would behave towards me. So, the man in the newsagent's might sell me the newspaper I ask for or he might ignore me or he might hand me a computer magazine. Or imagine what life would be like if all train drivers tossed a coin each morning to decide whether they would drive a particular train or not. Clearly, the rail service would not survive long, and the newsagent would soon lose all his customers. If the whole of social life was like that, social life would break down – indeed, it would no longer be 'social' at all.[4]

People could act in capricious ways if they chose to: but the newsagent does, in fact, hand me the newspaper I want because he has a living to make, and train drivers do generally drive trains, because they lose their job if they do not. People are free to choose, but choices are constrained, and people who possess the same resources and face the same constraints tend to (but do not always) make the same choice.

Extending the model

But is this model of choices made in a framework of preferences, resources and constraints really an accurate depiction of social life? Do we really make conscious choices about even the minutiae of everyday interaction? The answer, of course, is that we do not. The model we have described applies only to part of social behaviour, a part that Max Weber called 'purposively rational action'. For much of the time, we do not engage in a calculation of costs and benefits before we act; indeed, we do not experience the constraints on choices as constraints at all. It never occurs to the newsagent to do anything other than hand me my paper, just as it may never occur to me to drive through a red light. It is not the fear of prosecution that stops me from stealing; rather, not to steal is part of the morality that was instilled into me when I was a child. Constraints are *internalized* through socialization – the behaviour that they shape is taken for granted.[5] Nevertheless, the constraints are real, as anyone who tries to go against them discovers. For instance, people do not take shopping from another person's trolley in the supermarket. Strictly speaking there is no reason why people should not do this – the goods have not been paid for – yet it is not a course of behaviour that ever enters our thoughts. Anyone rash enough to attempt it, however, will quickly be made aware that the behaviour carries costs large enough to make it prohibitive![6] It follows that even though constraints are internalized, they may still be differentially distributed.

A further and closely related complication arises if we consider more carefully the relationship between resources, constraints, and action. We have been dealing with the set of objective constraints faced by individuals (whether they are aware of them as constraints or not). But if we want to understand why people behave as they do we need to focus on the constraints as they are perceived. Within the set of given objective constraints it is the subjective perception of constraint that is important if our goal is to account for observed behaviour.

A third complication concerns people's preferences, which, as we have already noted, can also vary. To return to marriage in Northern Ireland, it is unusual for Catholics to *wish* to marry Protestants and *vice versa*. In this case preferences concerning the religion of one's spouse more or less exactly match the most likely outcome. In the words of Pierre Bourdieu, 'the dispositions . . . inculcated by objective conditions (i.e. constraints) . . . engender aspirations (i.e. preferences) and practices objectively compatible with those objective requirements' (1977:77, parentheses added).

In other words, people prefer what they are most likely to be able to get.[7] While this may be true in many cases, it is not the whole story: the sour grapes principle does not always hold. Dissidents in the former Communist regimes of Central and Eastern Europe could not realistically have expected their preferences to be attained, but they held those preferences despite this. More generally, a society peopled by actors who only sought that which they were most likely to get would display a degree of quietism wholly uncharacteristic of modern societies. On the other hand, it is equally implausible to believe that preferences do not, to some degree at least, shape themselves to the restrictions of what can realistically be attained.

At this point, then, let us take stock. We began by presenting a simple model of the behaviour of social actors, in which choices were made between alternatives, given actors' preferences and the resources they possess and within a framework of constraints on action. We argued that this model could be applied to many areas of social life. Furthermore, resources and constraints are, we suggested, differentially distributed, so that different people face different costs and possess different levels of resources.

Then we extended the model by accepting that the idea of people actively choosing between alternatives is true of only part of social life. Much of what we do is unreflective, we do not constantly engage in the calculus of costs and benefits. Rather, people's behaviour is shaped by the processes of socialization through which constraints become internalized. The constraints are hidden, and only become evident when we go against them; most commonly, however, we do not. Nevertheless, it is still the case that these constraints of which we are commonly unaware are differentially distributed and thus provide the bases for an explanation of commonalities and differences in social behaviour.

We argued that people who share a common position in these respects will *tend* to make similar choices, while people who have a different position will be less likely to do so. This, in turn, gives rise to the empirical regularities that we observe in the social world and which, in a very basic sense, make social life possible.

We noted, however, that a satisfactory account of people's behaviour also requires knowledge of their preferences and of how they perceive the constraints on their actions. In practice we often observe more or less common behaviour among actors who share the same position with respect to objective constraints. This would seem to arise because, to the extent that preferences and perceptions of constraints vary, they do so in the same way as the constraints themselves.

The nature of constraints

We have been conceptualizing constraints on an action as deriving from the potential or likely cost of undertaking such an action. This simple idea is immediately applicable when we consider choices such as those involved in purchasing an item or when, for example, individuals seek to acquire jobs using educational resources. In other cases, however, these concepts become more complex.

In the case of money transactions, 'cost' is determined by price – each good has a price and its cost to us is what we have to give up in order to secure it. This idea can be extended to other actions: the cost attached to an action is what we have to give up in order to carry out that action (and secure the end to which it leads). In this example the element of constraint derives directly from the known cost: we are constrained to choose only among those goods we can afford. Similarly in the labour market: we can only hope to be considered for those jobs for which we possess the required qualifications.

However, costs often cannot be known exactly. In the case of someone who breaks a red light there is a probability, rather than a certainty, of being caught, and thus a chance of getting away with it. Or consider an economic example. In order to buy a house most people have to take out a mortgage: but the cost of this to them cannot be known exactly because (in some countries such as Britain) mortgage interest rates fluctuate.[8] Nevertheless, the idea is the same: the element of constraint derives from the expected cost of undertaking particular actions.

In many cases, costs are incurred whenever some *norm* is transgressed. In this way, norms also act as constraints. We use the term 'norm' in a very general sense to encompass all principles, ideas and expectations that express how social life should be carried out. In this sense, then, norms range from written laws through widely accepted 'rules' of behaviour, to expectations concerning behaviour. When a student comes to see a professor both have expectations about how the other will behave. By and large these expectations are not in any sense codified nor is either party explicitly aware of them. However, if these expectations are not met then there will be costs incurred. For example, if the student is rude the professor may not provide him or her with the favourable reference he or she is seeking. Conversely, if the professor does not behave in the way the student expects – if he or she is rude and aggressive – the costs to the professor are likely to be quite minor. While this is an example of the power differential that exists between professor and student, it also illustrates once again how the anticipated costs attached to the transgressing of expectations act to constrain behaviour.

However, it also exemplifies the point that the norms which underlie interaction are not only constraining: in a manner parallel to that in which assumptions about people's behaviour guide our own behaviour, so it is the fact that actors are knowledgeable that makes social life possible (only then can we speak of them as 'actors'). In other words, transgressing norms or rules will indeed entail costs, but knowledge of these (in what Giddens (1982:37) calls 'practical consciousness') is necessary for social behaviour. For example:

> When I utter a sentence I draw upon various syntactical rules . . . These structural features of the language are the medium whereby I generate the utterance. But in producing a syntactically correct utterance I simultaneously contribute to the reproduction of language as a whole. This view rejects the identification of structure with constraint: structure is both enabling and constraining. (Giddens 1982:37)

In our terms, the unconscious knowledge of syntactical rules constitutes a resource, but to transgress these rules will entail costs and thus the rules also constrain.

The relationship between actors' behaviour and the structure of rules and norms that we have been discussing is at the heart of sociological theory. It is obviously a mistake to see the two as distinct, to view norms as simply the external conditions of action. Norms change as do the costs attached to them, and this comes about through action. If the relationship between action and norms is deterministic, then we cannot account for such change. But if, as we have argued, actors do not have to act in accordance with constraints in a mechanical sense but, rather, are free to act in a variety of ways, bearing in mind the costs entailed, then the problem is not how to explain change, but, rather, how to account for stability. Since costs are relative (the cost of undertaking action X relative to the cost of undertaking action Y), a change in one part of the 'social system' can have ramifications for other areas. For example, if unemployment rises, actors may be more likely to resort to crime, not because the costs of criminal behaviour (in the sense of the probability of being apprehended and punished and in the sense of the norms and values which lead people to find crime morally repugnant) have changed, but because the alternatives, against which crime might be evaluated, are less attractive.[9]

A rule which is consistently broken cannot survive: thus repeated and widespread transgression of rules is likely to lead to their demise. However, two elementary but important points need to be made here. First, the ability to change rules is limited. While it is true that individual actions often establish what is considered to be appropriate behaviour (as in, say, the construction of gender identity in a particular setting), it is not the case that all constraints are equally susceptible to the effect of individual action in a given context. And, second, as we noted earlier, different actors have different capacities to bring about change in the rules.

The relationship between rules and behaviour is well captured in the analogy of a game of chess (see Bauman 1989:39; Elias 1978). At any given point in the game, moves can be made subject to constraints: different moves carry with them different costs, and what kinds of strategies are possible depends upon what resources are available. But the set of constraints within which a move must be chosen is itself established as a result of previous moves, and is, to some extent at least, an unintended consequence of previous moves which were made with an entirely different object in mind. The effect of a move by a particular piece on the structure of constraints may be limited or very far-reaching, and much will depend upon which piece is moved. A queen move will, in general, have greater impact than, say, a pawn move. In other words, moves (actions) are made within a structure that is the product of previous moves (actions) and which is reshaped by the moves (actions) themselves. Language provides one example of this process, as does the evolution of prices in a market. Prices change so that the cost of buying a good shifts over time, due to unintentional acts (the separate demands of many individuals cause the price to rise or to fall) and to intentional ones (as when, for example, speculators bid up or bid down the price of a security).

Stratification

We use the term *social power* to refer to an actor's position with respect to the resources he or she possesses and the set of objective constraints on action he or she faces. We could imagine that, at a given point in time, each actor could be seen as occupying a position of social power in some large (probably infinite) dimensional space, S, which is the space of all possible actions, no matter how trivial. Alternatively, we could ignore much of S and instead concentrate on a finite set of dimensions, $s_1, s_2, \ldots s_n$, which are of interest to us. We would then speak of each individual occupying a position of social power in each of these dimensions, relative to the positions of other actors. Thus we can think of different dimensions of social power corresponding to different sets of such actions. One way of approaching stratification might then be to define a stratum as comprising all those actors who share a common position of social power on some such dimension. In practice, such strata would be identified inductively by grouping together all those who had such a common position. This is a legitimate exercise: a good example can be found in the case of income, where we might identify 'income strata' with those households within each decile of the income distribution. However, in sociology, the study of stratification usually proceeds in the opposite direction. That is to say, strata are defined in terms of 'characteristics' of actors or the positions they occupy which lead to them sharing, to a significant degree, a common position on one or more dimensions of social power. Hence we speak of age stratification or gender stratification or class stratification, implying that, on average, those in a particular age group (or gender or class) will enjoy a common position of social power *vis-à-vis* those in another age group (or gender or class) on some particular dimension(s) of action.[10] In this sense, when we speak of stratification in sociology we are really referring to the bases on which actors come to occupy differential positions of social power. It follows, then, that an important task of stratification theory is to explain precisely how these bases, or structuring factors, come to give rise to these differential positions.[11]

It therefore becomes important to distinguish two things. The first of these is the degree of commonality in positions that different individuals enjoy, and the second is the degree to which actors share common bases of social power. It could be argued that no two actors share an absolutely identical position with respect to the resources they possess and the set of constraints on their actions. However, in the study of stratification we are concerned with what is usually called 'structured' social power, that is to say, the social power that is part of specific roles or positions in society, rather than idiosyncratic social power that an individual might possess. Such structured social power is then, in turn, seen as deriving from what we have called the bases of social power.

A common position on one of these bases can exist as what we term an *objective*[12] commonality, recognized by an analyst or observer (such as a sociologist) or as a *subjective* commonality, in which it is recognized by the actors themselves. This distinction, which we shall return to in our discussion of Marx and Weber in Chapter 2, is closely linked to a number of debates about the very nature of sociology as an enterprise. In our view it is important to attend to both types of commonality.

Traditionally, and deriving particularly from Marxist theory, the link between individual action and class position, for example, has been seen to arise through the growth of subjective awareness of class position. This is captured in what Pahl (1989:711) has called the 'mantra' of 'structure – consciousness – action'; in other words, actors themselves become aware of the role played by their common class position in structuring their social power and the consequences of this. But whereas Marxism viewed the development of a 'class in itself' as part of the historical process of societal transformation, other approaches (following Max Weber) have seen this as contingent and thus problematic (Bendix and Lipset 1967; Giddens 1973). On this account there can be no assurance that 'individuals holding similar positions within the class structure will thereby automatically develop a shared consciousness of their situation and will, in turn, be prompted to act together in the pursuit of their common class interests' (Goldthorpe and Marshall 1992:383). Whether or not this occurs is a question for empirical analysis.

The primary importance of stratification arises because the dimensions of stratification are the bases on which social power is distributed. However, an actor's class, gender, race, and so on are also linked to differential 'forms of consciousness'. We use this expression to refer to subjective perceptions of constraints and individual preferences. How forms of consciousness are generated is a topic beyond our scope, but the work of Bourdieu, referred to earlier, suggests a mechanism linking them to objective material conditions of action.

Class stratification

Thus far, then, we have sought to explain what we mean by 'stratification' on the basis of a model of the behaviour of individual actors. Individuals are located within a framework of social power of which they may or may not be aware. Their position of social power derives from the resources they possess to enable them to undertake particular actions and the constraints on so doing which they face. These resources and constraints exist as phenomena in the real world independent of individuals' own perceptions of them. Strata are, then, groups of actors who share, to a significant degree, a common position on one of the structural bases of social power, and thus have at least a partial commonality of social power.[13]

We now turn to the question of what distinguishes class stratification from the other possible sorts of stratification. The answer is that, usually (and speaking in very general terms) classes are defined on the basis that the members of a class obtain their livelihood in a similar fashion.[14] Different class schemes use different criteria for establishing this similarity, and we will be looking at these in Chapter 3, but most sociological class schemes invoke criteria of similarity that concern relationships between classes. For example, 'Classes are sets of structural positions. Social relationships within markets, especially within labour markets, and within firms define these positions' (Sorenson 1991:72). Similarly, Erikson and Goldthorpe (1992b:29) refer to classes as aggregates of social positions 'that are identified in terms of relationships within labour markets and production units'. In other words, the criteria arise out of, or seek to encapsulate, distinctions that exist in the organization of markets and the processes of production in modern society.

Strictly speaking, classes are conceived of as sets of positions, as the preceding quotation from Sorenson makes clear, rather than as the individuals who happen to fill them at any particular time. In speaking and writing of classes, however, we often refer to them as though they comprise the individuals who occupy the positions. This is a form of shorthand that is probably essential to avoid tortuous sentences, but it should be kept in mind that the underlying model is one in which classes are defined as aggregates of positions.

A simple example of such a class schema is a two-class Marxist model using the criterion of ownership of productive assets to define the classes. Here the two classes are made up of those who own the means of production (such as factories, businesses, shares) and receive their livelihood in this way, and those who do not and are therefore obliged to sell their labour power in order to subsist. In this case the classes are defined on the basis of relationships found within the process of production. Empirically, then, classes are defined as aggregates of occupations that are believed to share some specified common features. In turn, these common features give rise to a partial commonality of position for the people in these classes in terms of the constraints they face, particularly those that are salient for what are usually called, following Max Weber, 'life chances' or, as Erikson and Goldthorpe (1992b:239) express it, 'experiences of affluence or hardship, of economic security or insecurity, of prospects of continuing material advance, or of unyielding material constraint'.

The centrality of class as an explanatory concept in sociology derives from beliefs about its importance. Crompton (1993:120) for example, states that 'the work individuals do remains the most significant determinant of the life-fates of the majority of individuals and families in advanced industrial societies.' Similarly, class position can be shown to be related to a variety of other behaviours, such as the way people vote and their tastes and preferences in the area of consumption. Finally, classes are also believed to be collective actors *in potentia*; that is, class position (classes in themselves) is considered to be a possible basis for the formation of social groups who act to further their common interests through some sort of collective action (in other words, classes for themselves). In our view, class analysis – or, indeed, any other form of stratification analysis – should be concerned both to demonstrate the existence or otherwise of the link between these outcomes and class position (or, more generally, stratum) and to give an account of how the criteria used to define a class (or other stratum) give rise to these outcomes.[15]

How many bases of stratification?

A long-standing debate in the social sciences concerns how many dimensions of stratification can, or should, be identified. At its simplest the question at issue is whether there are one or several significant dimensions of stratification in society. Here Marx and Weber are often seen as representatives of the two positions: Marx stressing the overriding importance of class stratification, Weber allowing for the possibility of multiple bases of stratification in society. We discuss the ideas of Marx and Weber in more detail in Chapter 2; however, the debate concerning the number of bases of stratification was certainly not resolved by either of these two and it continues to this day. At its crudest the argument is whether there is one important basis of stratification (usually social class, but sometimes gender or race) or whether there are several.

Our belief is that this is an empirical, rather than a theoretical question. The number of bases of stratification is potentially infinite because of the range of possible human actions. Which dimensions of action we should focus on (and thus which bases of stratification will be relevant) depends, ultimately, on what we believe to be important for the purpose at hand. For example, people who are left-handed share a common position on certain dimensions of social power and can often face genuine difficulties in existing in a right-handed world. Few people, however, would argue that this is the most important basis of stratification in modern societies. On the other hand, there may be certain circumstances in which it is very important. Thus, a question such as 'what is country X's stratification system like?' is not very useful, since most countries will possess a variety of stratification systems, each of which may be important in different contexts.

Sociologists focus upon particular stratification systems – such as class and gender – because they believe that the consequences or outcomes to which they give rise (namely the differential distribution of social power relevant to certain sorts of actions) are of particular importance. Such an assessment of importance can be made on at least three, non-exclusive, grounds. First, we might argue that certain dimensions of social power are important from a political perspective: a focus on greater equality between people in their material conditions of life will lead inevitably to a focus on the distribution of life chances and the bases of stratification which underlie this. Second, we might argue that certain consequences of stratification have particular salience for people within a given society: once again, most people in modern societies are concerned about their standard of living and the kind of life they can give their children (if they have them) and so forth, and on this basis we would also want to focus on life chances and the forms of stratification – notably class – that underlie them. Third, we can argue that particular structural bases of stratification are especially important in understanding a society and how it evolves through time. For this reason we might be interested in class stratification not because we necessarily had any commitment to, say, increased equality in society, but because we believed such stratification to have consequences for people's behaviour in many other spheres (such as their voting behaviour) which, in turn, plays an important role in understanding the society and the social processes occurring within it. A Marxist perspective provides a good example. Marxists may be personally committed to the securing of socialism and the removal of class differences in society, but Marx's focus on the relations between capitalists and workers also provides the basis for understanding the workings and dynamics of capitalist society and, so Marx believed, its eventual transition to socialism.

We can, therefore, consider individual actors as being members of many, cross-cutting, strata. We might envisage them as occupying a particular cell in a multidimensional table, cross-tabulating all the possible bases of stratification one against another. We cannot focus on all these dimensions: our choice is determined by our particular concerns. It may be, indeed, that for some purposes only one dimension of stratification is important – in which case we would be focusing on the distribution of actors across one of the margins of this hypothetical table. However, in the majority of circumstances, this is unlikely to be adequate to account for some particular set of actions or outcomes. In looking at how people vote, for example, social class is usually important, but it is not the only dimension of stratification that plays a role here. Likewise, if we are looking at, say, educational attainment, then once again class stratification is important in accounting for variations in this but, in many countries, so also are factors like gender and ethnic or racial group.

Furthermore, the structural bases of social power, such as class, gender or race, taken singly or together, will always provide only a partial explanation of particular actions and their results. There are several reasons for this, but one of the most important is that an individual's social power is also the product of his or her individual history and circumstances (including chance events) which are independent of any of the bases commonly identified. However, precisely because such factors are idiosyncratic they tend to lie outside the domain of the study of stratification. By contrast the importance of the structural bases of social power lies in the fact that they provide a link which relates the organization of society to the behaviour of individuals. So, the sociological study of stratification is, in our view, the investigation of the 'inter-connections . . . between historically formed macrosocial structures, on the one hand, and, on the other, the everyday experience of individuals within their particular social milieux, together with the patterns of action that follow from this experience' (Goldthorpe and Marshall 1992:383).

Conclusions

We have used this chapter to try to set out the basis of our approach, working from first principles in models of individual behaviour. Since we have summarized our argument at various points throughout the chapter we do so only briefly here.

Constraints and resources are differentially distributed in society. Actors who share a common position with respect to resources and the set of constraints on a particular action or set of actions can be said to share a common position of social power. The sociological study of stratification deals with the bases on which this comes about; that is to say, strata are defined in terms of 'characteristics' of actors or of the positions they occupy that lead to them sharing, to a significant degree, a common position of social power. Thus, depending on what characteristics we can identify, there could, in theory, be many dimensions of stratification. Equally, however, there can be many dimensions of social power, since there exist very many kinds of actions that actors might seek to undertake. We also suggested that the various bases of stratification, which as well as shaping the distribution of social power, also play a role in shaping forms of consciousness. In other words, our definition of stratification is phrased in terms of the objective distribution of resources and constraints (and thus possibilities). But we would also argue that the actor's position on the bases of stratification will also, to some degree, help shape his or her perception of the objective constraints and the preferences he or she holds.

Which dimensions of stratification sociologists seek to study then depends upon which dimensions of social power – what sorts of actions – they are interested in. So, for example, a great deal of interest has been shown in economic constraints on actions or actions which are concerned with 'life chances', and the commonly cited forms of stratification – class, gender, ethnicity, age, and so on – are all, it is argued, bases on which to a greater or lesser extent life chances (among other things) are distributed. Traditionally, however, social class has been seen as the most important basis for the structuring of these particular kinds of inequalities, and in this book we follow that emphasis – hence this is a book about class stratification.

Notes

1. The power of the rational choice approach comes from the assumption of 'optimizing' behaviour (Coleman and Farraro 1992: xi). Given the set of preferences, costs, and constraints, actors are assumed to be rational and thus to 'optimize' their choice of actions (where optimize is defined, for example, in terms of making choices which maximize 'marginal utility').
2. People also have different preferences, which is something we turn to later.
3. This follows because the sides are numbered one through six and, if the dice is unbiased, each side will be face up the same number of times as any other face. Hence the average score of the dice (calculated over a large number of throws) will be the average of the values on the six sides of the dice – which is three and a half.

4. The work of Max Weber, in both *Economy and Society* and *The Methodology of the Social Sciences* provides an early statement of arguments of this sort.
5. Such action is called, by Weber, 'traditional action' and most activity is of this type – in other words, shaped by habits and customs.
6. Some of the best examples of people uncovering hidden constraints are found in the well-known work of Garfinkel (1967).
7. This is what Elster (1989) calls the 'sour grapes' principle: actors do not want what they cannot have.
8. In economics the problems that arise in this area are studied under the heading of 'decision making under uncertainty' (see, for example, Machina 1987).
9. And in turn this will trigger off further consequences. For example, if more people resort to crime, then the probability of being apprehended will decline as the police's workload increases. The government may then respond in one or more of several ways – by increasing the strength of the police or the severity of sentences (more custodial sentences and longer prison terms). In turn either of these will increase government spending, thus creating pressure for expenditure reductions in other areas or increased taxation or state borrowing. Any of these courses of action will then entail consequences, and so on.
10. This does not mean that there cannot be variation in social power among actors within a particular stratum – within a particular class or ethnic group or gender, say. Rather, it means that when we come to examine the distribution of a particular set of constraints in the population, distinctions of class, ethnicity, and gender should be evident. This is another way of saying that differences between strata should be significantly greater than differences within them.
11. In other words, it is not enough to demonstrate that a relationship exists between stratification on some basis and a particular dimension of social power: there must also be an adequate explanation for it.
12. Although we use the term 'objective' we nevertheless recognize that the sociologist's specification of resources and constraints is not 'objective' in the sense of being independent of theory. Objective constraints certainly exist but 'we must always speak of them and know them under particular descriptions, descriptions which will always be to a greater or lesser extent theoretically determined' (Bhaskar, quoted in Outhwaite, 1987).
13. It is only partial because such people, although they may be of the same class, for example, may differ in their location on the other bases of social power – they may be of different ethnic groups, age groups or genders.

14. But this is by no means universally accepted as the work of Burawoy (to be discussed in Chapter 2) and Przeworski (Przeworksi and Sprague 1986; see also Wright 1989b:297) illustrates. For these authors, the objective delineation of a set of classes is almost beside the point: rather, classes are constituted by the consciousness of individuals or the strategies pursued through collective action.

15. In the simple Marxist model such differences in life chances arise because the relationship between the two classes entails the exploitation of the non-owners by the owners.

CHAPTER 2

STRATIFICATION THEORISTS

Introduction

The study of stratification boasts an enviable pedigree within sociology. Virtually all the central figures in the development of the discipline were concerned to some degree with stratification, and for many it was the primary focus of their work. And today stratification and social class remain the objects of a great deal of theoretical and empirical endeavour on the part of sociologists. Later chapters of this book examine the application of approaches to the study of social class derived from current theorizing. In this chapter we begin to lay the groundwork for that by considering the work of a number of theorists of social stratification, selected on the basis of their relevance to the core issues around which debates in the area currently revolve. Thus we deal first with the so-called 'classical' theorists – Marx and Weber – and then with such contemporary writers on the topic of stratification as Michael Burawoy, Anthony Giddens, John Goldthorpe, Frank Parkin, Richard Scase, and Erik Olin Wright.

The classical theorists: Karl Marx

One characteristic of late capitalism is the explosion of choice that it offers to the consumer. This phenomenon is rarely better illustrated than in the vast array of books and articles that present, explain and interpret the writings of Karl Marx and, to a lesser extent, Max Weber. We do not wish to widen this wealth of choice by providing a comprehensive review of their work. Rather, our aim is to present a summary of the ideas of Marx and Weber as they have been carried forward to influence contemporary approaches to stratification, and, especially, class. We do this because, to a very considerable degree, these two writers established the context that continues to shape contemporary debate. In particular, we want to draw out two issues that retain particular importance in the study of stratification. These issues were highlighted in Chapter 1: they are, first, the distinction between what we called an objective and a subjective commonality of position; in other words, the distinction between the fact (recognized by an observer) of a group that shares a common position on one of the bases of social power and the recognition of that fact and its significance by the members of that group themselves. And the second issue concerns how many bases of stratification can be said to exist in society. So in dealing with each issue we will be concerned to show how the broad approaches to stratification adopted by Marx and Weber illustrate the framework that we developed in Chapter 1.

For Marx, a historical era or epoch is defined by the way in which, characteristically, people gain their livelihood: in other words, the mode of production. So, in societies like ancient Greece and Rome, the mode of production was based on slavery. In the Middle Ages there existed the feudal mode of production, while in Marx's own time, and ours, we have the capitalist mode of production. All pre-capitalist modes of production were essentially based upon agriculture, and here what Marx called the means of production were mainly land, domesticated animals and the tools of agricultural production. The capitalist mode of production, however, is essentially based upon manufacturing, and here the means of production are factories, offices, machinery, and investment capital.

According to Marx, each mode of production has associated with it a set of relations of production; in other words, in order to produce, people have to come together in the process of production and thus enter into relations with one another. At its simplest, Marx's argument is that, in all modes of production, individuals enter into these relations as a member of one of two possible groups or classes. One class owns the means of production while the other is forced to sell its labour power in order to subsist. But both groups are necessary for production. So, in the ancient world, the mode of production was slavery, the means of production was land, and the two classes were masters and slaves. In the feudal mode of production the means of production was again land, but here the classes were lords and serfs. In the capitalist mode of production, which is based on industry, the two classes are capitalists (or bourgeoisie) and workers (or the proletariat).

As Giddens (1973:27–8) observes, Marx often used the term class in a rather loose fashion, taking its meaning for granted. Nowhere in his work is there a concise statement of what exactly constitutes a social class and so Marx's views on class have been reconstructed by scholars drawing on a variety of his writings. For Marx, classes exist when the relationship of production is exploitative. By this he means that one group – which owns the means of production – is able to exploit the other. In slavery this exploitation is obvious. In feudalism it consisted in the serfs being obliged to provide free labour and/or a share of their produce to the lord. In capitalism it consists in the exploitation of labour by capital – that is, of the workers by the bourgeoisie. Marx argues that this comes about because the workers produce goods that are sold for more than the wages the workers receive. For example, a worker producing a good will receive a weekly wage – but what he or she produces in a week might sell for many times this. The difference between the two is what Marx calls 'surplus value', which is, once the capitalist's expenses such as maintenance costs and depreciation have been taken into account, the source of the capitalist's profit.

This leads to a situation, in Marx's view, in which capitalists become wealthier by accumulating profit derived from surplus value, while the proletariat are paid just enough to keep them healthy and able to function. Furthermore, Marx sees the work available under the capitalist mode of production as becoming increasingly oppressive. This is largely due to the increasing division of labour. What Marx has in mind here is that as mechanization grows and capitalist enterprises develop, individual workers will no longer produce anything specific: rather, each worker will do a specific job that contributes to the production of something. A car assembly line is a good – albeit more modern – example. No one working on such a line actually makes a car: one

Managers
workers

person fits the doors, another fits the engine, another super
the painting, and so on. Routinization and repetitiveness increase
as a result. For Marx, under capitalism workers become increasingly 'alienated' from their labour. This arises for three reasons:
first, workers have no control over what they produce – they
simply sell their labour, like any other commodity. Second, the
division of labour denies workers the satisfaction that they would
otherwise enjoy from producing something. Work does not satisfy
the desire to create something but instead it becomes an alienated,
external means to satisfy other needs. Lastly, increasing mechanization and routinization mean that, far from men being masters of
machines, it is the other way round.

A crucial element of Marx's model of class relations is its
dynamic implications. In his writings, Marx was much concerned
with explaining the way in which one historical epoch is transformed into another. According to Marx, while the specifics of
each transformation may differ, what they have in common is the
fact that each mode of production is eventually superseded
because of contradictions inherent within it. The same is true of
capitalism which will eventually be replaced by socialist society.
This will come about when the proletariat recognize themselves to
be a class and overthrow the bourgeoisie. In other words, when
class consciousness develops and the working class *in itself*
becomes a class *for itself*. Marx suggests a number of ways in which
this class consciousness will develop. For example, capitalism is
subject to periodic crises in which production outstrips demand
resulting in the laying off of workers and a further decline in
demand (because workers are also consumers whose net purchasing power is thus diminished). As the number unemployed ('the
reserve army of labour') increases, wages will be driven down, and
each of these periodic economic crises will last until wages have
been reduced to such an extent that it is once more possible for
capitalists to make profits from production. In such crises, Marx
argues, both capitalists and workers suffer, but the latter suffer
much more, and through this become aware of the difference in
interests of themselves and the capitalists as classes.

Marx points to a number of other features that are conducive to
the development of class consciousness, including urbanization
(which brings workers into geographical proximity) and the
tendency towards the homogenization of labour through the

Current economic system

Rising importance
of why the consumer
seeks sustainably designed
methods of produce/products

increased use of machinery – hence differences in skill between members of the working class will diminish. Marx also points to a tendency for so-called 'intermediate classes' to disappear as a result of the process of polarization in which large capitalist enterprises will drive out smaller ones, thus leading to the disappearance of groups such as the petty bourgeoisie (made up of small trades people, shopkeepers, artisans, self-employed workers, peasants). At the same time, the gap in relative material conditions between workers and capitalists will widen because of the continued expropriation of surplus value by the latter.

At the same time Marx recognized a number of obstacles to the development of class consciousness, of which the most important is the existence of a legitimating ideology by which the capitalist class provides a justification for the *status quo*. This arises because economic power and political power follow the same lines: thus, in Marx's famous phrase, 'the class which is the ruling material force in society, is at the same time its ruling intellectual force' (Marx and Engels 1965:61). In the work of later Marxist writers this phenomenon has become linked to the notion of 'false consciousness' – in other words, members of the working class can fail to recognize their true class interests because of false consciousness arising from the domination of what might be called the 'ideological means of production' by the capitalist class.

Marx presents this two-class model of capitalist society as an abstraction from reality; that is to say, a particular capitalist society will not in reality necessarily display the exact features of the model that Marx describes. Nonetheless, he argues that all such societies will develop towards this model. However, one major difficulty is presented by the existence of 'intermediate classes' lying between the workers and capitalists of capitalist society. We have already noted those groups that Marx believed would sink into the proletariat with the development of capitalism. However, he also recognized the existence of elements of the middle class that, far from declining, will actually increase in number as capitalism progresses. The clearest example is what we might nowadays call that section of the middle class whose members administer capitalist enterprises as managers, administrators or lower-level clerical workers who are indispensable to the functioning of production although not directly engaged in production themselves. As Goldthorpe *et al.* (1980/87:6–9), drawing on the work of Harris (1939) has noted, Marx's writings on this group contradict his statements about the polarization of classes under capitalism, since he quite clearly envisages these middle classes as expanding rather than becoming submerged in the proletariat.

Notwithstanding this, for Marx a class is defined in terms of its position in the relations of production: a class is thus not defined in terms of income, for example, since this is a consequence of class position, not a determinant of it. The same is true of occupation, narrowly defined: a self-employed plumber and an employee plumber share the same occupation and may earn much the same but belong to different classes. Position in the means of production, however, is extremely significant for Marx, since from it a range of consequences follow. As we noted, political as well as economic power follow these lines, and the whole dynamic of capitalist society is built around this fundamental exploitative division. The relationship between social classes is basic to understanding the entire workings of bourgeois society.

According to Marx, class does not refer to the beliefs that people hold about their position but to objective conditions. But Marx also saw class relations as existing at the political or ideological level. Hence the distinction between a class in itself – by which he means a group of people who share the same objective class position – and a class for itself, which is that group of people who recognize that they share the same class position and have the same class interests, which they may then try to further through, for instance, political action. In such a case we can speak of class consciousness.

The classical theorists: Max Weber

Weber, unlike Marx, was concerned with sociology as a discipline, and much of his work involves trying to develop the appropriate methodology and concepts for the study of society. For Weber, classes are defined in terms of differential life-chances. Under capitalism, life chances are allocated through the workings of the capitalist markets and, particularly, the labour market. A class, for Weber, is made up of all those who share a common situation in these markets. In a famous quotation he summarizes this view as follows: 'a class situation is one in which there is a shared typical

direct quotation

probability of procuring goods, gaining a position in life, and finding inner satisfaction' (Weber 1968:302). This probability of procuring goods and so forth then depends upon what people can bring to the markets of capitalism – hence Weber is concerned to define class in terms of individuals' resources rather than by reference to their place in the relations of production. But these resources only have value in the context of a market: hence class situation is identified with market situation. People come to the markets – commodity, credit, and labour – unequally. Where people possess a common set of goods, services, or skills for market exchange, a broadly similar standard of living and life experiences will be found. Dozens of such 'economic classes' may be discerned in a society at a particular point in time.

Much more focus to class than level of economic stability

But in any historical situation, Weber argued, economic classes combine into 'social classes'. Although economic classes are the products of impersonal market processes, other factors intervene to provide the continuity required to transform economic relationships into discrete social categories. Social mobility is the key to such a transformation: 'a social class makes up the totality of class positions within which individual and inter-generational mobility is easy and typical' (Weber 1968:302). Social classes are therefore perpetuated within families. These are the repository for key economic resources and the locus for mobility-related processes such as educational participation.

Weber argues that, in modern capitalism, it is possible to define four social classes each of which comprises *clusters* of economic classes between which mobility is common and easy, but between the social classes mobility is infrequent and difficult. In defining these four social classes Weber first distinguishes between those who own property or the means of production and those who do not. He then goes on to distinguish important classes within the propertied and the non-propertied, on the grounds that they have differing relations to the market. 'Class situations are further differentiated . . . according to the kind of property . . . and the kind of services that can be offered in the market' (Weber 1968:928). Among those with property he distinguishes between the 'dominant entrepreneurial and propertied groups' and the petty bourgeoisie, while among those who lack property, the market situation of those with formal credentials (the middle class) is distinguished from that of manual workers.[1]

Thus in contrast to some of Marx's views, Weber believed that the expansion of the middle class comprised of formally qualified workers would be characteristic of capitalism. The relationship between social classes is also characterized by attempts, on the part of members of such classes, to preserve their advantages relative to others through the exclusion of outsiders. Thus they pursue what are sometimes termed 'strategies of class closure' which include things such as the monopolization of credential-granting institutions (Waters 1991:150).

For Weber, class relations are one aspect of the distribution of power in society. He defines power as 'the probability that an actor will be able to realize his own objectives even against opposition from others with whom he is in a social relationship' (Giddens 1973:156). Power, however, is not synonymous with economic domination (Giddens 1973:44): it is more ubiquitous than this, as the foregoing definition makes clear.

Like Marx, Weber accepts that individuals who constitute a class may not recognize that they do. Whether members of a class recognize this fact or not depends on specific historical and cultural conditions. Indeed, Weber thought that what he termed status groups were more likely to figure in people's own consciousness than was class membership. By status groups he meant groups of people who share a common style of life and have a certain level of prestige in society. Status groups exist by virtue of the subjective evaluations (positive or negative) of others and their members are therefore conscious of the prestige or status that they have as a group. Whereas classes derive from economic factors linked to the resources people bring to the market, status depends upon the styles of life groups follow and the assessments made of them by other people. Put another way, status groups are based on relations of consumption, as opposed to classes which are based on relationships in production. As with classes, positively valued status groups seek to preserve their positions by limiting access to them and by restricting interaction with other groups in important areas (for example through marriage rules such as endogamy). For Weber, both status and class are possible bases for the formation of social groups in relation to the distribution of power in society (Giddens 1973:44).

Weber also pointed to the importance of party formation as another such basis. Party here means a group of individuals who work together because they have common aims or interests: thus it includes political parties but is wider than simply this, encompassing 'any group whose purpose it is to exercise power in society or which is concerned with the competition for power' (Hamilton and Hirszowicz 1987:14).

These three dimensions may overlap, in the sense that a social class may also be a status group, or a status group may constitute a party. Equally, each can cross-cut the other: so, for example, status groups may divide the members of a social class. However, none of these dimensions is in general wholly reducible to another. Status groups and parties occupy positions of power which do not rest on an economic basis *per se*.

If we compare Marx and Weber, we can detect a number of commonalities and divergences. On the one hand, they both agree that classes are rooted in objective economic conditions. They therefore distinguish between the existence of classes and the awareness of class membership and common class interests on the part of class members. On the other hand, Marx defines classes in terms of the relations of production whereas Weber defines them in terms of market situation. One way of summarizing this difference is to say that whereas Marx's emphasis is on the structure of positions available in capitalist society (of basically two kinds), Weber is more interested in the processes whereby different individuals are allocated to positions in this structure. Additionally, Weber rejects the Marxian emphasis on the relations of production as central to understanding the whole social formation. Classes are not the only significant sort of social group: in the course of history status groups and parties have displayed a significance that the Marxist concern with classes completely ignores.

Within sociology it is perhaps this last distinction that has most usually been considered to distinguish Marx and Weber, the former pointing to a single basis of stratification within society (namely class), the latter opening up the possibility of the existence of 'multiple bases for inequality' (Grabb 1984). However, as several authors have pointed out (Giddens 1973; Hamilton and Hirszowicz 1987 among others) to view class, status and party as different dimensions of inequality does not seem to accord with Weber's own views, at least when these dimensions are viewed as continuous rankings on which individuals (or families) can be placed – possibly high on some dimensions, low on others. Rather, Weber was concerned with the development of social groups: classes, status groups and parties are all groups which enjoy power, but in each case this derives from a different source. As we shall see, this distinction of views, one of which sees individuals or families ranked on one or more continuous hierarchical dimensions of stratification and another which focuses on strata conceived of as groups coalescing around particular positions of power in society, is evident in much writing on stratification even up to the present day.

'On the shoulders of giants': Class theory after Marx and Weber

Weber's death in 1920 ended the dialogue between the two giants of sociological theory.[2] Subsequent developments in stratification theory, and especially European class theory, are often viewed as being channelled through the different understandings of the social sciences put forward by Marx and Weber. Divergence between those channels expanded through the attempts by adherents of each theorist to maintain the essence of the founder's vision when responding to a rapidly changing capitalist system and global economy. Indeed, in some limited measure Weber's own divergences from Marx can be traced to the changing face of capitalism in the final decades of the nineteenth century and into the start of the new century.

What were those changes? Four transitions are noteworthy for the study of stratification. The first is the transition from competitive to monopoly capitalism (Grimes 1991:174). In the earlier, 'Heroic', phase of capitalism, an individual was the owner, employer, and manager of an enterprise. The bold entrepreneur was a significant presence in the life of ordinary workers, and the long-term destiny of a firm was tied to that individual's family. But the dispersed ownership fostered by joint stock companies renders the capitalist and capitalism abstract and depersonalized. A bureaucracy replaces the entrepreneur, and, 'the essentially dichotomous nature of class relations becomes hidden and accommodated within the hierarchical gradations of authority relations' (Scase 1992:10). This transition is a product of the second industrial revolution, which in the late nineteenth and early twentieth centuries created the new forms of communication and transportation that made possible mass production and distribution: 'These new high-volume technologies could not be effectively exploited unless the massive flows of materials were guided through the process of both production and distribution by teams of salaried managers' (Chandler 1984/92:133).

Second, the rise of mass social democratic parties in Western Europe, although not in the United States, gave the propertyless a voice in governance. Welfare capitalism became the dominant form of economic organization in the industrial world. Even in the United States by mid-century the capitalist system presupposed the existence of an extensive framework of state support, partly to capital and partly to employees. 'The wage contract ceases to be a private contract except on subordinate and accessory points. Not only conditions in the factory, hours of work, and modalities of contract, but the basic wage itself are determined outside the market' (Polanyi 1944:251). Social protection became a defining feature of advanced capitalist society in its generality, and, in the diverse forms that it can assume, fundamental to understanding the specificity of individual societies (Castles 1988; Esping-Andersen 1990).[3] Capital and worker were joined by the state as arbiters of wages and working conditions, and neo-corporatist arrangements moved economic issues into the political arena.

Third, the reach of capital increasingly transcended national boundaries. The globalization of capital added new twists and turns to ownership and management of the production process, further obscuring the relations between capital and labour. Administration and ownership might remain concentrated in a small number of core countries, but the operations of the major concerns were dispersed globally. This challenges the nation-specific understanding of stratification. For example, the American working class is proportionately the smallest in the world if restricted to US workers or the largest if the international employees of American capital are included in the relevant proletariat (Parkin 1979:27–8, footnote 7, commenting on the work of Nicos Poulantzas 1977:119).

Fourth, output came to depend less on the brute labour power of a mass of productive workers and more on the finesse of technical and support services (Scase 1992:17). The immediate consequence is a marked heterogeneity among the proletariat in terms of the quality of what they bring to the labour market. More generally, this transition within the capitalist system created a proliferation of categories that do not neatly fit into either a bourgeoisie or a proletariat. Differences among those selling their labour for wages could no longer be sensibly accommodated within a single working class. Indeed, categories of employees assumed vital roles in the capitalist enterprise and within the state sector.[4]

Weber confronted aspects of the first and last trends, but not the second or the third. In particular, neither Marx nor Weber anticipated the role that governmental institutions and policies would carry. Weber emphasized entrepreneurship (Maddison 1982:79), while 'Marx obviously felt that some institutional changes in property relations were necessary to launch the capitalist process, but that thereafter government policy played no directly sustaining economic role in his schema' (Maddison 1982:25).

The response to the complexities of the post-World War II period failed to meet the standards set by Weber and Marx. The Weberian common ground gravitated, or, more accurately, descended, towards a fixation on the divide between manual and non-manual workers. Misreading of Weber led to notions of stratification as composed of independently influential hierarchies, or continua, of class, status and 'power'.[5]

Marxist orthodoxy was less compromising, tenaciously insisting that, fundamentally, the class structure remains polarized. Considerable ingenuity needs to be expended to 'save the phenomenon' of a two-class society. The Marxist legacy, more than that left by Weber, was prey to disputing heirs: is one to be faithful to the early Marx, the later Marx, or the Marxism of the Second Internationale? A basic split divides Marxists who treat classes as collectivities – with the class as the unit of analysis – and those drawn to conventional social science approaches focusing on individuals as cases. Geography was a strong influence. The writings of Marx and Weber were late immigrants to North America and slow to assimilate. From early in the century the middle class in the United States seemed to offer more potential than did the working class for mobilizing change (Grimes 1991:174). Initially the United States, and, by the 1980s, social democratic Europe, confronted Marxist students of stratification with the twin problems of the expanding, and comfortably situated, middle class and the disappointing revolutionary raw material of the proletariat.

The contemporary authors reviewed here all seek to push stratification theory forward in ways that respond to twentieth-century trends. Some are more reverent than others to the ideas of Marx or Weber. Some seek to capture the generalities, while others are more empirically minded, both in the sense of a commitment to an interaction between data and concepts and in understanding specific societies.

In condensing the ideas of these writers, we continue for the moment the questionable practice of distinguishing by pedigree. Most contemporary writers on stratification are clearly strongly influenced by both Marx and Weber. Giddens and Goldthorpe, perhaps the most prominent 'Weberians', explicitly reject that restrictive label with which others seek to honour or mock them (Giddens 1980, Afterword: see also Wright 1989b:285, footnote 20; Erikson and Goldthorpe 1992b:37). And as Parkin (1979:25) notes, 'Inside every neo-Marxist there seems to be a Weberian struggling to get out' – at least if they feel the need to confront the complexities of advanced capitalism.

We focus on six authors. Scase and Giddens are more discursive and sweeping in their approach, the former as a neo-Marxist and the latter as a synthesizer and innovator. Erik Olin Wright and John Goldthorpe exemplify a more empirically minded strand to the study of stratification. Both have accumulated substantial bodies of work, representing two of the more sustained theoretically driven efforts to understand the dynamics of late capitalism and industrial society. Finally, Michael Burawoy and Frank Parkin represent somewhat dissident ways of thinking in, respectively, the Marxist and Weberian traditions.

The analytical Marxism of Erik Olin Wright

Contemporary Marxism is a house with many rooms, but few interior doorways. Structural Marxists occupy one of the larger of those rooms. They regard class as an objective location that is defined by the relations of production, which in turn establish the material interests facing persons occupying positions within that class. One assumption is that any person in such a position will think and act in a predictable manner, though the degree of assumed predictability varies among theorists.[6] Moreover, as persons change, or anticipate changing their class, their material interests simultaneously change. Poulantzas (1975) and other structural Marxists accordingly devote considerable energy and ingenuity to the task of mapping the class structure. In other words, they are betting on the explanatory power of knowing what is a 'class in itself'. This incurs a cost. They neglect, relative to other branches of contemporary Marxism, the evolution of class and class consciousness from shared historical experience within the capitalist system.

The most sustained effort at creating a structural Marxist theory that is both relevant today and loyal to Marx's nineteenth-century writings is that of Erik Olin Wright. Wright's central concern has been with the 'problem of the middle class' – that is, of its expansion and vitality as capitalism matured, to the embarrassment of Marx's predictions.[7] In doing so, Wright breaks with orthodoxy by seeking to understand capitalist society not by consulting texts but by constructing new theories and then testing their empirical utility in existing societies, primarily in his native United States.

Two basic solutions to the problem of the middle class have been advanced by Wright, subjected to self-criticism, and reformulation. Both build on the insight that there need not be a one-to-one correspondence between locations in a class structure and classes. Accordingly, Wright's expositions are constructed around the idea of contradictions. In his first class schema, certain occupations may stand in 'contradictory class locations': thus, a manager is simultaneously in the working and the capitalist class (Wright 1989b:301). We focus on his second response, which is found in his book *Classes* (1985).[8] Here, the contradiction stems from the multidimensional nature of exploitation: the incumbents of certain locations are both exploited in one dimension and exploiters in another. It follows that 'the class map is built around relations to exploitation-generating *assets* rather than exploitation *per se*' (Wright 1989b:306).

This requires some context. Classes are not formed by relations to the market but by the productive assets that a class controls, 'which lead them to adopt certain strategies within exchange relations and which thereby determine the outcomes of those market transactions' (Wright 1989a:14). To manage the leap from such abstraction to actual class locations, Wright works within a framework of 'analytical Marxism'. Importantly, in this the unit of analysis becomes the individual rather than the class and the labour theory of value gives way to a deductive strategy based on teasing out the implications of unequal property relations using game theory (Roemer 1982a and b[9]).

Exploitation is defined as 'an economically oppressive appropriation of the fruits of the labour of one class by another' (Wright 1985:77). Although for the time being classes remain the unit of analysis, such a formulation breaks with the more expansive orthodox Marxist view of exploitation since Wright is identifying exploitation through differences found at the level of distribution, not in relations of production. The difference is arcane, but vital to Marxist theory. In Marxism, 'capitalist appropriation is not exclusively or primarily an appropriation of *things*, but rather an appropriation of subjectivity, of working energy itself, of the physical and intellectual powers of man' (L. Colletti quoted in Carchedi 1989:108).

Wright also extends the Marxist formula of 'land, labour, and capital' to look at exploitation on the basis of four types of productive assets: labour power, capital, organization, and skills or credentials. Organization, the new kid on the block, is formally defined as the 'conditions of coordinated cooperation among producers in a complex division of labour' (Wright, 1989a:16). These four productive assets define four kinds of exploitation, each of which is associated with a single mode of production. The following pairs result: exploitation in terms of labour power is paired with feudalism, capital with capitalism, organization with state socialism, and skills with socialism. However, the world is not so easily portrayed: 'Since concrete societies are rarely, if ever, characterized by a single mode of production, the actual class structures of given societies will be characterized by complex patterns of exploitation relations' (Wright 1985:87).

What does this tell us about advanced capitalism? In his most recent published formulation, Wright (1989b:347) concludes that in contemporary capitalism skill exploitation and organization exploitation are *secondary* forms of exploitation, creating strata within classes built upon the primary dynamic of exploitation on the basis of capital assets. Inequality in ownership or control of any of these can constitute exploitation, but Wright pays particular attention to exploitation on the basis of organization assets.[10] This is important because ownership of organization assets is split between senior managers and capitalists, and is thus the basis through which Wright can claim that middle-class employees exploit other categories of workers.

Organization assets take on particular importance in understanding the class structure of state socialist societies. However, organization assets within advanced capitalism itself provide the dynamic with the potential to create massive change. This follows from the fact that the central contradictory location within contemporary exploitation relations is that of managers and state bureaucrats: 'They embody a principle of class organization that is quite distinct from capitalism and that potentially poses an alternative to capitalist relations' (Wright 1989a:27).

Overall, Wright's formulation does respond to the concerns described in Chapter 1 as central to stratification:

> common class interests, then, mean that people in a given class, by virtue of their relationship to the underlying mechanism embedded in the social relations of production, objectively face the *same broad structure of choices and strategic tasks* when attempting to improve their economic welfare. (Wright 1989b:282, emphasis added)

Wright's work also exemplifies what Parkin (1979:x) terms 'professorial Marxism', aimed at an audience of the already initiated and of new recruits among students at elite institutions of higher education. The use of arcane language is not unknown in bourgeois sociology, but Wright's approach to class structure, currently embracing 12 classes, is clearly the stuff of which dissertations and not revolutions are made. This is perhaps inevitable when one strives to be faithful to Marx's writings, yet takes as one's unit of analysis the individual rather than the class (Carchedi 1989:125).

Bringing workers back in: Michael Burawoy and production politics

The writings of Michael Burawoy represent a very different strand of Marxist class analysis from that adopted by Erik Olin Wright: class as shared *work* experience. Other theorists, notably E. P. Thompson (1968) stress the process by which shared life experiences – including neighbourhood, family, and culture broadly defined, as well as the workplace – underpin class identity. One basic schism within contemporary Marxism is between those who, like Wright, strive to understand the dispersion of objective interests within the class structure and those who, like Burawoy, are more concerned with classes as nodes of common identity.[11] The anaemic state of class consciousness in the 1980s and 1990s would seem to make such a 'processual' perspective on class formation unpromising theoretical terrain.[12] Yet Burawoy both narrows the base of the processual perspective to encompass the work setting alone and applies it to the very contemporary problem of why state socialism, not monopoly capitalism, lies in history's dustbin.

First, what is distinctive about Burawoy's general perspective on class? Class here is explanatory because it 'determines the subjective conditions of conflict, above all the identities and meanings of those engaged in conflict' (Wright and Shin 1988:59). So class is learned. Where is it learned? It is learned within the capitalist enterprise. To Burawoy, 'the character of the capitalist enterprise itself created a distinctive class consciousness, irrespective of the consciousness carried in from outside' (Burawoy and Lukács 1992:4). The essence of a class is the consciousness within the workers, rather than a position in a class structure with attributes that automatically adhere to anyone residing in that position.[13]

Burawoy's definition of the process of production is expansive, viewed as a production regime. Basically, this refers to 'the organization of work and its regulation', the lived experience in production that, to Burawoy, provides the link between a class in itself and a class for itself (Burawoy and Lukács 1992:113). A more formal statement distinguishes two shaping factors:

> First, the organization of work has political and ideological *effects* – that is, as men and women transform raw materials into useful things, they also reproduce particular social relations as well as an experience of those relations. Second, alongside the organization of work – that is, the *labour process* – there are distinctive political and ideological *apparatuses of production* which regulate production relations. (Burawoy 1985:7–8)

A focus on 'relations in production' within the work setting – and indeed the use of the term 'factory regimes' in the title of one of his books – is indicative of Burawoy's iconoclasm among neo-

Marxists. The factory has been dismissed as a relic of 'Fordist' modernity, at least in the capitalist core countries. Perhaps Burawoy's atypical interest in stratification within state socialist countries sustains his focus on the workplace in a period when others strive to be relentlessly post-Fordist and post-modern.[14]

This leads to an intriguing possibility: that the capitalist production regime generates consent on the part of workers, while that of state socialism generates dissent. There are two related steps to this argument. First, centralized appropriation is visible, while capitalist appropriation is dispersed and opaque. This explains the passivity of the working class, however defined, across the range of capitalist societies and epochs (Burawoy and Lukács 1992:112–13). Second, each method of appropriation is associated with workplace practices that shape the meaning of work. Let Burawoy and Lukács speak for themselves:

> Capitalism appears natural and inevitable because the private appropriation of surplus is hidden. By contrast, under state socialism, the central appropriation of surplus is transparent and therefore has to be legitimated. Here the state is the self-declared appropriator of surplus. It is the transparent oppressor and exploiter, making its appearance in production as a triple alliance between managers, union, and party. (Burawoy and Lukács 1992:147)

The legitimating ideology is that of Marxist-Leninism. It is 'embedded in a constellation of rituals in the workplace, such as communist shifts, production conferences, brigade competitions, production campaigns, and so on. Precisely because workers have to act out the virtues of socialism, they become conscious of its failings' (Burawoy and Lukács, 1992:147).

Richard Scase: A pragmatic Marxist

The legacy of Marx is given a less self-conscious, and certainly a less cumbersome expression, in the work of Richard Scase. His perspective is of interest because it represents a broad strand of contemporary theorists who claim a primary debt to Marx, are concerned with empirically tracking and comprehending the changing face of capitalism, but are more interested in generalities about classes than in precise maps of class structure and in which individuals fall within which class.

For Scase, class theory speaks to 'essentially exploitative and antagonistic productive relations: producers of surplus and non-producers who own means of production' (Scase 1992:5). Scase observes that notions of social class are largely absent from everyday discourse, although social scientists continue to proclaim the centrality of class for understanding social processes and outcomes (1992:4). This is because occupations are what we can see and experience in ordinary life. Non-Marxist sociologists miss the point because they, like the public at large, are fixated upon occupational distinctions. To Scase, occupations are products of class relations.[15] Class relations may have changed since Marx's day so as to proliferate the number of occupations, but the fundamental bipolar class dialectic remains the essence of capitalism even in its current phase. Beneath the calm surface of welfare capitalism, Scase argues, the imperatives of capital continue to define the essential features of advanced capitalist societies. What are to Scase the minutiae constituted by differences in attitudes, life styles, and life chances can be relegated to explanation at the level of occupation. The big picture, though, requires an understanding of class structure (Scase 1992:26).

Scase is, as a result, able to speak rather loosely about classes and class relations, without agonizing about his ability to define mutually exclusive categories to which specific persons can be assigned. To pursue his argument, Scase instead offers the concept of strategic management. The central dynamic of contemporary capitalism is expressed by the concept of strategic management, which is the exclusive province of owners (or delegated owners) who formulate corporate or institutional policies. Operational management, in contrast, confers no direct relationship to capital. Therefore, the class placement of engineers and technical workers creates no anxieties for Scase comparable to those with which Wright suffers in his work. Their role is to enhance the value of capitalist investment. Ultimately, then, Scase is arguing that class relations are expressed in terms of control, and that the same dialectic of antagonistic employment relationships is active in retail enterprises and state bureaucracies as in manufacturing industry (1992:23). The superficial and trivial role he allocates to occupations follows from this: 'occupations do not determine the nature of social classes; instead, it is class relations, embedded as these are within the control relationships of organizations, that determine the delineation of occupations and, therefore, occupational orders' (1992:25–6). Further, to Scase, classes have not proliferated, as they have for Erik Olin Wright. Occupations have proliferated as capitalism matured; classes have not. Indeed, Scase views classes as inherently antagonistic although their members may not recognize it. In part, this is because of the distraction that occupational differences create.

A bipolar class structure is generic to capitalism. 'The development of capitalism in different Western countries has produced similar patterns, in the expression of both class relations and stratification systems . . . Any differences between countries are but variations on a common theme' (Scase 1992:30). The picture is not entirely uniform however. Sweden's historically powerful labour movement is credited with mitigating the worse excesses of the market without infringing upon personal freedom (1992:76–8). Although Scase is a more orthodox Marxist than Wright, he is also less dogmatic in remaining on the barricades. Scase (1992:89) thus concludes his essay on a sombre note: 'It is the rise and fall of state socialism which the twentieth century has witnessed rather than the demise of capitalism. The question is no longer whether or not capitalism but of what variety or type.' In essence, capitalism has stumbled into a compromise in which its class contradictions are no longer life threatening. Scase's reformist realism would be heresy to Wright, who takes a less sanguine view. But it is important to note that by locating distributional and similar issues in the realm of the occupational order, Scase manages to remove Marxist class theory from the embarrassment of the greater explanatory power of Weberian class categories (see Chapter 3 below) and, at the same time, to explain the woefully limited rallying power that class affiliation now possesses.

Frank Parkin's bourgeois critique of Marxist class theory

Parkin (1979) seeks to reinvigorate the Weberian approach to stratification. Relations between classes are to be understood as 'aspects of the distribution of power' rather than as mere differences in material living standards. The ownership of capital is to be treated seriously as a distinctive source of inequalities. Overall,

Parkin's work offers a useful counterpoint to depictions of class that assume either contradictory or harmonious class relations.[16]

Parkin concedes that the anaemic model of class offered by modern mainstream sociology fed the attraction of Marxist theory during the 1960s and 1970s. The divide separating manual from non-manual workers did not give stratification the centrality it merits within social theory. Restating, and substantially condensing, Weber's ideas on class, Parkin seeks to offer a more robust alternative. The potential is inherent in the 'human raw material of class analysis that Weberian usage designates as "actors", thereby singling out the role of conscious agency and volition . . .' (Parkin 1979:4). This means that positions in the class structure are occupied by individuals who differ on grounds other than their role in the production process. To Erik Olin Wright, these are unimportant details: the class position a person currently occupies essentially tells us all we need to know about their interests and potentials. Parkin points to the potential for gender and ethnicity – and indeed other attributes – to form the basis of exploitation *within* a social class.[17] More generally, when permitted conscious agency and volition, individuals within a class can seek to improve their situation relative to the dominant class through what Parkin identifies as two methods of social closure. These are, first, processes of usurpation, through which actors seek to improve their position relative to that of the dominant class; and, second, processes of exclusion directed against segments of their own class. Fewer resources and less effort are required to exclude a 'visible and vulnerable minority group' than to challenge a dominant class: thus the fractured working-class characteristic of capitalist societies arises not through 'false consciousness' but rather as a rational response on the part of workers (Parkin 1979:95).

Parkin's reformulation of the Weberian position is expressed in these two methods of social closure, exclusion and usurpation. All forms of exclusion are exploitative according to Parkin. Property and credentials are the two most common forms of exclusion, and the principal beneficiaries of exclusion are viewed as 'constituent elements of a single dominant class' (Parkin 1979:58). Usurpation is the response to exploitation, collective action directed at retrieving some or all of what exclusion yields for the dominant class (or ethnic group or gender). The strike is the archetype of usurpatory action, expressing both the potential power and practical limits of what usurpation can achieve. Given those practical limits, the attractions of exclusion as a form of closure within the working class are clear. Exclusion on the basis of race, ethnicity, or gender reaps concrete returns for its practitioners. Like other forms of exclusion, this proceeds along lines established by the state:

> It is *never* the case that exclusionary criteria are simply plucked out of the air in a purely arbitrary manner. In all known instances where racial, religious, linguistic, or sex characteristics have been seized upon for closure purposes the group in question has already at some time been defined as legally inferior by the state. (Parkin 1979:95)

Parkin thus builds a theory of class and a portrait of contemporary class structure based on Weber's concern with processes of social closure through which groups (classes among them) defend their interests. In his reading of Weber, class relations are inherently fraught with tension – but a tension which is sustaining rather than destructive:

> The Neo-Weberian position advanced here is that the relation between classes is neither one of harmony and mutual benefit, nor of irresolvable and fatal contradiction. Rather, the relationship is understood as one of mutual antagonism and permanent *tension*; that is, a condition of unrelieved distributive struggle that is not necessarily impossible to 'contain'. (Parkin 1979:112)

What defines a class is the mode of collective action that it typically deploys to accomplish or contend with closure. Property ownership and credentialism are associated with very different bases for exclusion and usurpation, and, thus, very different countering strategies by the groups at which they are directed.

The notions of tension, closure, and exclusion afford Parkin considerable flexibility when approaching the topic of stratification. This is entirely consistent with Parkin's conception of what stratification theory represents – a 'special package of concepts for carrying out the exercise of making things intelligible' (1979:114). Societies are too complex and too varied to make structured social inequality a subject for elegant or generic explanation. Parkin offers concepts as tools, and claims only that for the purposes at hand they are more useful than alternative approaches. So no universal principles or laws are advanced. Societies must be understood on their own terms, not as examples of this or that economic system. Such immodest modesty is highly Weberian. It is immodest because it stakes such a wide claim to what it can explain. It is nonetheless modest in its recognition of the legitimacy of competing views and in looking at the specific rather than the universal. In practical terms, it means that Parkin, like Scase, is not concerned to perfect a set of classes into which individuals can unambiguously be assigned membership.[18] And, like Scase, he can claim easy relevance to the situations of advanced capitalist, late capitalist, and non-capitalist societies alike. Parkin's construction of Weberian stratification, though, offers an unusually wide and substantial bridge from class-based stratification to that based on gender, ethnicity, and race. It is, however, a bridge that remains little used. Parkin's work is notable more for its witty rejoinder to the presumptions of Western Marxism in the 1970s than as the foundation for inquiry.[19]

Anthony Giddens and class structuration

The Class Structure of the Advanced Societies is Giddens's contribution to what he regards as '*the* problem in sociology: the question of classes and class conflict' (1973:19). His answer is both novel in its core ideas and systematic in its presentation. Fundamentally, the answer requires revisiting one of the 'blank spots' in Weber's work, 'the processes whereby "economic classes" become "social classes", and whereby in turn the latter are related to other social forms' (Giddens 1973:105). This leads to the notion of class structuration: the degree to which the class principle has become entrenched in a specific society.

The spark of novelty that Giddens brings to class analysis is evident in his concept of exploitation. Exploitation is 'any socially conditioned form of asymmetrical production of life chances. "Life chances" here may be taken to mean the chances an individual has of sharing in the socially created economic or cultural "goods" which typically exist in any given society' (1973:130–1). Exploitation is therefore expressed through differentials in market capacity, rather than through surplus value. Now in most respects, the use of such a definition of exploitation makes a theorist *persona non grata* in the neo-Marxist camp. But it is important to note that in some respects Giddens's approach is more expansive than, say, Erik Olin Wright's. In particular, to Giddens rewards are not limited to material goods for consumption but extend to the faculties that allow for the use of rewards generated in the market. Class differences therefore encompass tastes and abilities.

Such an approach to exploitation causes Giddens to stress the link between market capacity and other bases of exploitation that become embedded in class structure and which, indeed, serve as that structure's cement. Market capacity comes in three basic forms: property, credentials that attest to the possession of certain knowledge and skills, and manual labour power. To the extent that these capacities are each linked to closed patterns of intra- and inter-generational mobility, the result is a three-class system that is typical of capitalist society: an 'upper', 'middle' and 'lower' (or working) class. The class structure of a particular society depends on the distinctive combination of what Giddens terms mediate and proximate structuration factors. Mediate factors are those that 'intervene between the existence of certain given market capacities and the formation of classes as identifiable social groupings'. Proximate structuration captures the 'localised' factors that condition or shape class formation. Three sources of proximate structuration are highlighted. Two operate within the productive enterprise: the division of labour and authority relationships. The third source of proximate structuration is forged in consumption patterns, as in the emergence of class-specific residential areas. Overall:

> to the extent to which the various bases of mediate and proximate class structuration overlap, classes will exist as distinguishable formations. . . . *the combination of the sources of mediate and proximate structuration . . . creating a threefold class structure is generic to capitalist society.* But the mode in which these elements are merged to form a *specific class system*, in any given society, differs significantly according to variations in economic and political development. (Giddens 1973:110)[20]

Giddens claims that the consequence is both a three-class model and a corresponding stable disparity in life chances (although the specific phrase used is 'economic returns') between those classes (1973:41–50). Class structuration, however, needs to be understood in terms of the dynamic of advanced capitalism. This requires attention to the mutual dependence of capital and the state. Capitalist enterprise presupposes a framework supplied by the state. The state relies on resources, through taxation and borrowing, that are located in the private sector, and over which it has but scant influence. And, to varying degrees, persons are aware of these contradictions within the capitalist system and act accordingly (Giddens 1984:310–19).

This parallels Giddens's treatment of class structuration. The potential for conflict is both generic to capitalist society and differently expressed in each specific society according to the convergence of contradictions and the intersection among various interests. Classes are the primary embodiment of contradictions within capitalism, and thus the primary basis of stratification and source of conflict: 'Capitalism is a class society, and the contradiction between "private appropriation" and "socialized production" is locked into class divisions which in turn express opposing interests' (Giddens, 1984:317–18).

John Goldthorpe: The demographics of class formation

The approach to class stratification associated with John Goldthorpe is central to one of the more sustained intellectual projects in contemporary sociology: an exploration of the nature of industrialism and its social concomitants, particularly the relationship between economic growth, industrialization, and social mobility. Goldthorpe's initial approach is grounded in Lockwood's (1958) concepts of market situation and work situation and an understanding of how those combine to form social classes. Market situation refers to categories whose members are known:

> to be typically comparable, on the one hand, in terms of their sources and levels of income, . . . in their degree of economic security and . . . chances of economic advancement; and, on the other, in their location within the systems of authority and control governing the processes of production in which they are engaged. (Goldthorpe *et al.* 1980/87:40)

This is the foundation for a body of ideas and related inquiry that grows in sophistication and finesse.[21] In essence, Goldthorpe and his colleagues link the structure of positions associated with a particular form of the division of labour with the imprint made on that structure by social mobility and the extent to which it facilitates class formation. Goldthorpe's work elevates the study of mobility into the central component of 'demographic class formation' (Marshall *et al.* 1988:22), suggested but not systematically explored in the writings of Giddens, Parkin, and, indeed, of Weber.

In *The Constant Flux: A Study of Social Mobility in Industrial Societies* (Erikson and Goldthorpe 1992b) the claims made for social mobility's importance to class stratification are established through a broadly comparative study. That study examines two sets of issues:

> on the one hand, those of how the mobility of individuals also reflects the structural aspects of economic development and, on the other, those of how mobility rates, as both endogenously and exogenously determined, help to create or to undermine the conditions under which class identities are formed and class interests pursued. (1992b:32)

Class structure is conceived as being built around differences in the employment relationships inherent in positions and the resulting schema is designed specifically for the purpose of studying social mobility 'within the total populations of mid-twentieth-century industrial nations, both capitalist and state socialist' (1992b:37). This requires, or prompts, some modifications to the basic market situation/work situation model. An initial threefold division of class positions is put forward as common to Marx and Weber based on employment relations: employers, self-employed, and employees.

The structural component of class is then elaborated in two main senses. First, property has become transformed into corporate or state-owned forms so that most 'major' employers are organizations. Consequently, Goldthorpe looks to a broadly defined service class rather than to a class of employers as the primary embodiment of property ownership in the class structure.

Second, the number of employees has continued to expand and the differentiation among them of relations to their employers has also increased. Several key consequences for class structures follow from this. One is that wage employment through a labour contract is distinguished from service employment within a bureaucratic context where trust, rather than direct supervision, governs employee activity. Briefly, the employment relationship enjoyed by staff differs from that of workers. Another consequence is that positions among both staff and workers differ in ways that represent distinct class positions. Some staff are unambiguously in a service relationship and for others that relationship is 'attenuated'; some workers are granted little autonomy and discretion, while others must be granted some aspects of a service relationship. The employment relationship for several categories of workers might be considered as being 'intermediate'. This is characteristic of routine non-manual positions 'which exist, so to speak, on the fringes of professional, administrative bureaucracies' and of the 'lower-grade technical and first-line supervisors'. Each set of intermediate positions constitutes a class in the Erikson and Goldthorpe schema (1992b:43). Their market situations differ, but from the employer organization's viewpoint their work situation is in part staff and in part labour (Erikson and Goldthorpe 1992b:40–4).[22]

Mobility patterns by and large determine the nature of these classes and their role in society. In addition to the emphatic role of social mobility, this approach to stratification argues strongly for the centrality of class in the creation and perpetuation of structured social inequality. It also supports the treatment of class as an attribute of families rather than individuals (see also Parkin 1971:14) and makes the nation-state the logical unit of analysis: demographic and political factors specific to each society govern the extent of class formation that is present. Finally, class structure is tied less to capitalism than to industrial society.

Pedigree and theory

'If I have seen farther, it is by standing on the shoulders of giants' is the humble aphorism often attributed to Sir Isaac Newton (Merton 1993). The continuing stature of Marx and Weber as thinkers on stratification surely stems from their comprehensive understanding of the relationship between stratification systems and historical epochs.

Generally, those who seek to take in the big picture are best able to maintain a direct and faithful link either to Marx or to

Weber. The greater the desire to understand a specific society or to be systematically comparative, the more evident the imprint of a dual pedigree. Erikson and Goldthorpe (1992b) and others such as Lockwood (1958), regard themselves as standing astride the shoulders of both Marx and Weber:

> the opposition between Marxian and Weberian conceptions of class that is by now enshrined in sociology textbooks is in many respects exaggerated, and especially in view of the fact that the work of neither author can be regarded as providing a canonical statement of his position. (Erikson and Goldthorpe 1992b:37, footnote 10)

We, too, do not wish to advance reverence to the dead as a virtue in theory construction. Rather, we want to look at what contemporary stratification theory has to say concerning the two key issues that framed the beginning of the chapter: What distinction is to be drawn between an objective commonality of position and a subjective commonality of position? How many bases of stratification can be said to exist in society?

Most contemporary theorists continue the effort to understand the processes that translate class relations into categories for collective awareness and action. Scase is an exception in abandoning the search for a 'class for itself', conceding that occupation, rather than class, is the locus for self-identification in advanced capitalism. This obscures the basic underlying dynamic of class relations. For those continuing the search for a self-aware class, that search has become more an act of faith than the product of solid evidence. Giddens, for example, describes the conditions under which class awareness should be maximal, but his ideas have not generated a research literature that supports those contentions.

Perhaps some of the resulting embarrassment to class analysis is self-inflicted. By phrasing the question of objective or subjective commonality of positions as an all-or-nothing proposition, theorists set researchers an impossible task. This is particularly true if we, like Parkin (1979:4), look at the individuals who constitute a class as possessing 'conscious agency and volition'. Members of a class can thus simultaneously engage in usurpatory forms of closure against another class and exclusionary activity that fractures their own class. In short, we can each have several, indeed many, objective and subjective commonalities. The one that will be dominant depends on how the bases of social power are configured in a society and on the specific consequence or outcome in which we are interested. This complexity is awkward for those who invest considerable theoretical capital in the presumed instability of contradictory class locations:

> Social groups, no less that individuals, appear to be quite capable of acting upon general principles, which at some level of abstraction, seem so apparently at odds as to lead only to self-annulment or paralysis. Contradictory class locations, as with so many of the widely advertised contradictions of capitalism, seems to be especially glaring in the immaculate realm of theoretical construction but noticeably less troublesome to those being theorized about. (Parkin 1979:110)

To us, this reinforces the need to build class analysis on top of a solid foundation that explains the behaviour of those individuals.

The question of objective versus subjective commonality of position relates to the second issue raised early in the chapter, the relationship between class and other bases for stratification. Parkin, for example, dampens expectations for finding strong class awareness by detailing how status groups intersect with, and thus obscure, class boundaries. Race, ethnicity, gender, and culture are all potential suppressers or amplifiers of class-based stratification. The intersection between, and interaction among, alternative bases of social power remains for the most part a weakly developed aspect of stratification theory, despite the contributions of Giddens and Parkin. Their work offers insight into how the relative force of these bases of social power varies among societies, but theory is again often a poor guide as to where and when one will be dominant in practice.

Conclusion: What a theory of class should tell us

Much contemporary thinking about social class has its roots in capitalism's most dynamic phase of economic growth: roughly the years 1950–73 (Maddison 1982). It only recently became clear that the post-1973 economic stagnation represents a new phase of capitalism. To some, the new phase makes the study of social classes obsolete. We will return to that contention in Chapter 7 armed with evidence accumulated through a series of chapters that form the empirical heart of this book. Those chapters explore the themes that command the attention of contemporary class theorists. Chapter 4 looks at the class structures that emerge when we apply different theoretical class schemata to specific countries. In Chapter 5, we examine the frequency of social mobility between classes, and ask whether the results support the belief that some countries are more 'open' than others. Chapter 6 turns to the issue of whether stratification systems can be extricated from the specific context of nation-states and dealt with more generically. It is clear that the emergence of welfare capitalism changed the nature of class relations substantially from that characteristic of the historical periods with which Marx and Weber were concerned. Welfare capitalism, however, takes on many forms. This tends to strengthen the extent to which class structures are distinctive to the society in which they are located.

But after parading the core ideas of two classic and six contemporary theorists of class so swiftly we clearly need to make some critical and evaluative judgements before moving on.[23] Class is central to sociology because of its potential as an explanatory concept. Our yardstick for comparing rival contemporary theories is therefore the degree to which they can explain the consequences experienced by individuals on the basis of differences in the social power that they possess. What are those consequences? We can, we believe, usefully distinguish three sorts of consequences or outcomes. The first might be described as apparently *unconscious* or largely *involuntary*. An example would be class differences in morbidity and mortality; another would be the development of preferences and tastes linked to class position. A second set of outcomes comprises *conscious* or voluntary behaviour but which is not *class-conscious* behaviour. In other words, class members may behave in similar ways without requiring that we invoke the argument that they must share a consciousness of their common class position. Rather, the behaviour of class members is similar because, to a significant degree, they share a position of social power, and their behaviour arises as a response to this. And third, we can point to *class-conscious* outcomes. These are the consequences that arise when class members act out of an awareness of their common class position: a class becomes a class for itself.

These three outcomes, then, are what, in our view, a class theory should explain – and by this we mean that such a theory should explain not only why, in a given instance, some such outcome arises, but also why, in other instances, it fails to arise. But to produce a yardstick that tells us the efficacy of alternative theories of class stratification requires a metric associated with the adequacy of explanation. First, can it be shown that there exists an association between class and the kind of outcomes we have enumerated? Second, can it be demonstrated how the characteristics that are used to define class positions lead to such outcomes? This latter is by no means a trivial requirement since it entails explaining the mechanisms by which the characteristics used to define classes work through to the observed consequences.

That an association exists between class position and various outcomes is very well attested to. However, when we turn to the specification of the exact mechanisms by which class position is linked to these various outcomes, matters become less clear. This is because there are, in fact, two issues that need to be considered here. First, since class concerns the differential distribution of rewards, a theory of class must start by showing how class position gives rise to differential rewards. And second, the theory must go on to show precisely how differential material rewards give rise to a range of differential outcomes.

To summarize: the yardstick we want to use to compare class theories starts from the axiom that class is a concept that is useful insofar as it explains certain sorts of outcomes. The adequacy of the various explanations advanced by a theory then depends upon the degree to which they demonstrate that there is an *association* between class position and outcome; and upon their providing an account of this association that links class position to differential rewards and differential rewards to outcomes. Our yardstick is, then, very much an *empirical* measure, insofar as it asks whether or not what the theories say is supported by the empirical evidence.

On this basis it is perhaps immediately apparent that some theories cannot fare well simply because they have been advanced without the support of empirical analyses. This is particularly the case with Giddens, Parkin and, to some degree, Scase. This is not to say that their work has not been useful: indeed, quite the contrary. A good example is Giddens's (1973) discussion of class structuration. Although he himself did not seek empirically to test the adequacy of his ideas about class structuration, the concept, and the terminology, are both widely used and discussed in the study of class stratification. And the same can be said about Parkin's notions of social closure. It remains the case, however, that their ideas are not specified in a manner that has led, or is likely to lead, to major empirical endeavours.

Of the three empirically orientated approaches we have examined there is a distinction in terms of both the outcomes that are of primary interest and the nature of the explanation. Here Burawoy's approach represents a sharp contrast to those offered by Goldthorpe and Wright. Burawoy probably takes the prize for the clarity with which class is associated with the particular outcome of greatest interest to him, namely class-conscious behaviour – but fares less well when other outcomes are at issue. Clarity comes at the expense of comprehensiveness here, because Burawoy's theory fails to account for the distribution of differential unconscious or voluntary outcomes. Workers experience particular relations in the production process which Burawoy has explored as a participant observer in various work settings, but there is no obvious way for these observations to be linked to anything other than a bifurcated class structure of managers and workers. Class, for Burawoy, is a state of mind that translates into action and as such exists only in the consciousness of individuals.

Wright also singles out class-conscious behaviour as the key outcome. While Burawoy sees class as process, Wright views it as a structure. What is important to Wright for all three types of outcomes that we have specified as the yardsticks for evaluating class theories is the individual's location in an objectively defined class structure. Wright's explanation, though, of how location in the class structure comes to be linked to differential rewards is cumbersome because it must be constructed within the self-imposed strait-jacket of soliciting the approval – never forthcoming – of orthodox Marxists.

Goldthorpe's approach also offers a class structure defined *ex ante*. As such it fares best when the consequences at issue are either unconscious or the result of behaviour that is voluntary but not class conscious. Indeed, Goldthorpe's concept of class structure successfully associates class location and rewards, such as the possibility for mobility to a more favourably situated class location. His class schema also appears to have more explanatory power than Wright's for a range of outcomes (Marshall *et al.* 1988). However, while Goldthorpe's approach allows us to identify the consequences of the occupation of particular class positions, he shares with Wright a certain weakness in demonstrating the mechanisms whereby this occurs.

The approaches of both Wright and Goldthorpe are also weak in explaining the conditions under which class action will arise from common class consciousness. This is perhaps to be expected: the study of classes for themselves has, of late, found itself in somewhat barren terrain. As a practical matter, class consciousness may be difficult to engender since, empirically, it may be difficult for actors to discern the effects of this particular basis of stratification when these bases are numerous and cross-cutting in their effects. What we observe and experience are the consequences of occupying a particular set of positions of social power and this may serve to obscure the effects of a particular form of stratification. Class consciousness will arise only when actors have a reflexive awareness of the link between class position and outcome. All things being equal this is perhaps more likely to occur when class is one of a very small number of factors that influence social power. What is much more likely is that those who share a common position of social power (rather than a common position on one of the bases of stratification) or common outcomes (such as a common set of preferences) will recognize their common interests. Thus the often remarked upon growth in the importance of groups that form around single issues and the shifting set of allegiances to such groups that individuals will have over their lifetime.

Notes

1. Weber's writings, like those of Marx, do not offer posterity a concise, authoritative statement concerning the principles of stratification. Other sections of *Economy and Society*, for example, contradict or dilute the clarity of the passages cited above on economic and social classes.

2. It is a misrepresentation to characterize Weber's work as a reply to Marx. As Giddens (1971:123–4) notes:

   > When Weber wrote his first works, he took his point of departure from the contemporary problems which dominated the mainstream of German economic history and jurisprudence . . . Nonetheless, it is true to say that the conclusions which Weber reaches in these early studies increasingly

channelled his concerns into avenues which brought him into direct relation
with the areas in which Marxist thought was concentrated: in particular, the
specific characteristics of modern capitalism and the conditions governing
its emergence and development.

3. Thus, 'party' became an element of Weber's famous triad of 'classes',
   'status groups', and (political) 'parties' as the 'phenomena of the
   distribution of power within a community' (quoted in Parkin 1971:46).
4. Other changes undermined the surface simplicity of stratification
   systems in the mid-nineteenth-century capitalist societies. For example,
   the demise of the landed nobility in the decades after World War I
   eliminated a distinct system of social honour in European stratification systems based on inheritance (Parkin 1971:39). And the drama of
   the tensions between the old aristocracy and the *nouveau riche* faded
   into obscurity.
5. Noteworthy examples include the 'city studies' of W. Lloyd Warner
   and the Lynds and, more recently, the status attainment tradition
   associated with Blau and Duncan (1967) and Sewell and Hauser
   (1975). Grimes (1991) chronicles the fortunes of class analysis in
   American sociology.
6. Wright and Shin (1988) offer a clear but succinct contrast between
   'structural' and 'processual' approaches to class, and insight into why
   Marxists often appear to talk past one another in contemporary
   debates.
7. It would be more accurate to say that the extent of that expansion
   belies Marxist expectations; Marx can be read as anticipating a
   growing complexity of the class structure and enhancement of the
   middle class's position within that structure ('the trend of bourgeois
   society': cited by Bottomore 1991:14 in reference to the 'later' Marx).
   Elsewhere, Marx observed that the growing supply of workers with
   white-collar credentials, through universal public education would
   lead to the 'devaluation' of those very credentials (see Edgell
   1993:66). A related problem is the revolutionary potential of the
   middle class, a potential that might prove the counterbalance to the
   disappointing record of the working class in changing capitalism.
8. Wright's work is distinctive in its tenacious and self-critical development. The virtues of this approach, as well as considerable clarity of
   exposition, are most evident in Wright's (1989b) essay 'Rethinking,
   Once Again, the Concept of Class Structure'.
9. These articles and books appeared while Wright worked on what was
   to become *Classes* (1985). They fuelled a self-critical assessment of
   the neo-Marxist theory that Wright's work had relied upon since his
   first published work in the field of stratification (Wright 1976).
   Kamolnick (1988) offers an ill-tempered critique of the result,

but extends his critique to Wright's earlier work as a further example of the evils that follow from subsuming Marxism within sociology instead of practising it as an alternative to neo-Kantian 'bourgeois social science'. Contemporary Marxism is fractured to a degree that precludes reference to a fair-minded surveyor of the scene or even a broad canvas such as that offered by Mills (1962). However, Carling (1991) compiles a useful primer on analytical Marxism.

10. The notion of exploitation via organization assets provides leverage for consideration of the class position of both managers in capitalist enterprises and state bureaucrats under either capitalist or state socialist regimes.

11. Thompson's portrayal of the early history of the working class is viewed as 'classic' but unorthodox because of his tenacity in looking at identity centred around the shared experience of resistance to capitalism rather than the, albeit forced, accommodation to the logic of capitalist development (see Burawoy 1985:77, footnote 65).

12. Processual approaches stress that 'class is an embodiment of the past in the present', while structural approaches look at the objective choices facing individuals in which 'class is an embodiment of possible futures in the present' (Wright and Shin 1988:59).

13. It may seem odd to cite Erik Wright as an authority on Burawoy's perspective, which is so different from that advanced by Wright throughout the last 20 years. But the article in question is one of the clearest statements of the difference between structural and non-structural versions of Marxist class theory. Moreover, the acknowledgements and footnotes of Burawoy and Wright evidence a continuous dialogue between the two, however different their conceptions of contemporary Marxism. Wright and Shin (1988:59) translate that difference into the language of rational actors thus: processual approaches express the preference orderings of the actors themselves, while structural approaches look at the 'feasible set of actions that exist independently of the motivations of the actors'. In our view as given in Chapter 1, class theory needs to address both preference orderings and opportunities.

14. Burawoy's reading of change in capitalism does, however, focus on a sequence of factory regimes (see Burawoy 1985:261 for a summary of his interpretation of this scenario and how it relates to the themes of post-modernism).

15. As, in his view, are all aspects of stratification: 'Stratification systems reflect the control relations that constitute the core elements of class structures' (Scase 1992:27).

16. This elaborates a position Parkin staked out in 1971 in his *Class Inequality and Political Order*, a radical Weberian critique of inequality

in the capitalist core countries. His subsequent work extends the ideas as a more direct counterpoint to the Marxism that rose to prominence during the 1970s and to alter the balance given to occupation, on the one hand, and property on the other. Parkin (1971:19) represents 'the backbone of the reward system' as a hierarchy of (six) broad occupational categories, but supplements these fairly conventional distinctions by elaborating on the view that 'to characterize the occupational order as the backbone of the reward structure is not to ignore the role of property, but to acknowledge the interrelationship between the one and the other'(1971:24).

17. The perspective of John Goldthorpe, to which we turn next, high-lights the importance of the class of origin as a source of difference among those occupying a common current class position.

18. Parkin is dismissive of neo-Marxist efforts to define class boundaries:

> Since classes in the full Marxist sense are collectivities forged in the heat of political struggle, and since the contours of this struggle never correspond to the boundaries of the class model, the effort expended in constructing such a model seems to fall squarely within the commonsense meaning of unproductive labour. (Parkin 1979:27)

19. Parkin (1979:115), for example, describes Western Marxism as a 'permanent dress rehearsal' for the 'grand explanatory performance' on which the curtain never seems to rise' and notes that 'Inside every neo-Marxist there seems to be a Weberian struggling to get out' (1979:25).

20. At this point in the text Giddens alludes to the situation of societies that are not culturally and ethnically homogenous. Here it is import-ant to note that for Giddens the class principle becomes an especially potent basis for structuration when it coincides with status group membership.

21. Landmark studies include the 'Affluent Worker' project (e.g. Gold-thorpe *et al.* 1969) and the Oxford Mobility project (Goldthorpe *et al.* 1980/87), as well as the more recent comparative mobility project with Erikson (Erikson and Goldthorpe 1992b). Each set of studies is supported by a substantial intellectual foundation anchored in journal articles and essays (see Clark, Modgil, and Modgil 1990 for an energetic exchange of views concerning that body of work).

22. Erikson and Goldthorpe thus confront the same issue that Scase considers through the concept of 'strategic management' but conclude that a two-class model cannot represent the implications for class structure.

23. We would, of course, argue that the six we have chosen are representa-tive of the main avenues of contemporary thought on class. We have deliberately omitted some writers who feature consistently in earlier

texts – notably Ralf Dahrendorf (1959) and Gerhard Lenski (1966). This is because we believe that, to a degree, what has survived in sociology of their distinctive contribution to the study of stratification has been absorbed by, and included within, the work of the authors discussed here.

CHAPTER 3

CLASS CLASSIFICATIONS

Introduction

Among the six contemporary theorists of class discussed in the previous chapter, there exists an obvious division between those who consider it necessary to begin by delineating a class structure in some detail (Wright and Goldthorpe) and those who do not (Burawoy, Parkin, Giddens and Scase). The research programme characterized by the approach of the former authors is often called 'class analysis' (Goldthorpe and Marshall 1992). Put simply, this is the empirical investigation of the consequences and corollaries of the existence of a class structure defined *ex ante*. The volume of investigation in that programme is by now very substantial indeed.[1]

Stratification is the study of the bases on which social power is distributed. We therefore agree with Goldthorpe and Wright on the need to begin with a definition of class structure into which each family and individual can be unambiguously classified. This has merits even if we do not propose to undertake empirical research using class as an explanatory factor. The process of classification forces us to be concrete in our thinking about exactly what constitutes a class and who belongs to it. This chapter therefore offers a kind of 'how to' guide, setting out the main problems encountered when empirically distinguishing social classes and then detailing how first Wright and then Goldthorpe resolve them.

Although the class schemata of Goldthorpe and Wright are of central significance in sociology, they are probably less familiar to most people than those class classifications used in government statistics or by market research companies. Can we not simply adopt those classifications, so bypassing the problems of constructing new class schemata? The answer is no: official class schemes do not find favour with class analysts for reasons that we briefly note here.

Official class schemes

In many countries statistics collected by government or other public bodies relating to characteristics of the population are often broken down according to some official set of 'class' categories. One of the best known of these is the British Registrar General's five-category classification, which distinguishes the following strata:

1. Professional occupations.
2. Intermediate occupations.
3. Skilled occupations.
4. Partly skilled occupations.
5. Unskilled occupations.

Frequently class 3 is split into non-manual (3N) and manual (3M) occupations, and the Armed Forces are sometimes included as a sixth category (Marshall *et al.* 1988:20).

Although the Registrar General's scheme is almost always referred to as a 'class' classification this is a misnomer, since it was originally intended as a means of grouping occupations that share a common prestige or standing within the community and, since 1980, it has been presented as a grouping according to occupational skill.[2] In this sense the Registrar General's scheme is not a class classification at all, unless we take occupational skill as our criterion for the definition of classes. But this would be somewhat *ad hoc* insofar as there is no theory which would justify the use of such a definition of class. Furthermore, the allocation of occupations to classes is apparently made on the basis of judgements on the part of the Registrar General's staff (Marsh 1986), rather than in accordance with any explicit theory.

The Office of Population Censuses and Surveys (OPCS) assigns individuals to classes as follows:

First, they are allocated an occupational group, defined according to 'the kind of work done and the nature of the operation performed'. Each occupational category is then assigned 'as a whole to one or other social class' . . . Finally, however, persons of particular employment status within occupational groups are removed to social classes different to that allocated to the occupation as a whole. (Marshall *et al.* 1988:19–20, parentheses added)

As might be anticipated, this procedure leads to some problems, not least in a high level of inconsistency in the allocation of individuals to classes (Leete and Fox 1977). This stems from the somewhat imprecise definitions of the classes and of the procedures for assigning occupations to them which are, so Marshall *et al.* 1988:21 suggest, the consequences of the atheoretical basis of the scheme.

Theories and structures

There are important points of agreement and disagreement in how to move from class theories to maps of class structure. Points of agreement include that we are mapping positions, not persons; that the family is the appropriate unit of class composition; the top of the class structure of capitalist societies is too small to isolate easily as a separate category; and that the comparative study of class structure needs to incorporate the distinctive position of those in the agricultural sector.

First, then, class structures are usually regarded as being formed by positions rather than by persons. The class structure comprises 'empty places' (Wright and Perrone 1977) and dramatic changes in which persons occupy particular positions may occur without altering the shape of the class structure.[3]

However, an obvious difficulty arises insofar as not everyone occupies one of the positions that comprise a class structure; put more simply, not everyone has a job. Children are the prime example, but the same holds for retired people, the unemployed, and women who do not engage in paid work outside the home. Does this mean they cannot be assigned to a class? The answer to this is no. The unemployed are generally allocated to a class position on the basis of the job they previously held, as are the retired (where this is relevant). The cases of women who do not work outside the home and of children are treated somewhat differently. Under what is sometimes called 'the conventional view' (Goldthorpe 1983) it is families, not individuals, who are regarded as the basic unit of class analysis. This convention has been widely accepted (see, for example, Giddens 1973:107, footnote 5, and Wright 1978:92). Thus the problem is one of assigning families or households to a class. So, children and women without a paid job outside the home are assigned a class position derived from that of the main income earner. Typically, then, a married woman will be assigned to a class determined by her husband's occupation. On the other hand, while this approach allows us to assign a class to children and to women who do not work outside the home, it presents some difficulties when applied to dual-earner families, such as those in which both husband and wife are working. In such cases retaining the family as the unit of class analysis requires that the 'dominance' approach be used (Erikson 1984). This assigns the family to a class based on the occupation of whichever working person is considered 'dominant'. Erikson takes the dominant person to be whichever one has the job which has the greater impact on the life chances of the family (Erikson 1984:504–5).[4] So, a job requiring high qualifications dominates one requiring a low level of qualifications; non-manual dominates manual work; professional employment dominates self-employment which in turn dominates work as an employee, and so on. Applying these principles, Erikson arrives at a dominance ordering of jobs. In practice, however, the application of this and similar dominance orderings classifies families in a way which differs little from what emerges from the 'conventional' approach, since, in the vast majority of cases, the 'dominant' job is the husband's.[5]

Third, a feature of the class structures that are drawn empirically is that they typically do not include a 'peak'. The primary reason for the absence of a 'haute bourgeoisie' is that property was transformed during the course of the twentieth century into corporate forms, and consequently most employers are organizations not persons (Erikson and Goldthorpe 1992b:40–1). Those persons who are characterized as 'large' proprietors in fact operate rather modest enterprises by the standards of late capitalism (Marshall *et al.* 1988:54–9) and are far removed from the levers that run the capitalist economy. The tendency for organizations, rather than entrepreneurs, to stand at the top of the capitalist system is intensified in peripheral countries where most large-scale enterprise is foreign owned (Mouzelis 1986). Erik Olin Wright is an exception to this tendency, defining a grand bourgeoisie that consists of those owners of the means of production who employ 10 or more paid workers.

Finally, most of those drawing maps of class structure for industrial societies find it useful to distinguish between the agricultural and non-agricultural sectors.[6] This is particularly true for comparative studies. Farmers represent between 1 and 25 per cent of the positions in the class structure in industrial societies and agricultural labourers between 1 and 14 per cent (Erikson and Goldthorpe 1992b:328, 353).[7]

Constructing and reconstructing Wright's classes

As we noted in the previous chapter, Erik Olin Wright has produced two class schemata, which we will label Wright I and Wright II. Both of them are attempts to retain the essence of a distinctively Marxist approach to class analysis coupled with a recognition of the greater complexity of class structures which has evolved since Marx's time. Thus, both approaches make use of the concept of contradictions, and display a subtlety and originality which seem to have evaded many of Wright's critics.

The starting point for understanding both Wright class schemata is that any given social formation will contain more than one mode of production. So, in developing his first class schema (presented in Wright 1976) Wright notes that, in advanced capitalism, simple commodity production exists alongside the capitalist mode of production. According to Wright, in such societies it is the petty bourgeoisie (that is, self-employed workers) who are engaged in simple commodity production, and thus they constitute one class in Wright I. Within the capitalist mode of production there are the conventional two classes – the bourgeoisie and those whom they exploit – the proletariat. However, these three classes are clearly not exhaustive of all those engaged in production in modern societies, and Wright argues that there also exist three 'contradictory class locations', which are of two

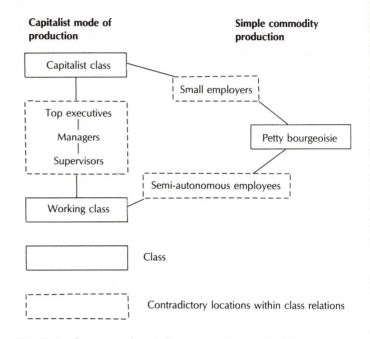

Figure 3.1 Basic class map of capitalist society (Source: Wright 1985: 48).

kinds. First, supervisors and managers are in a contradictory class location since they fall between the bourgeoisie and the proletariat in the capitalist mode of production, being simultaneously dominators of the proletariat (as agents of the bourgeoisie) and themselves dominated by the bourgeoisie. Second, there are two classes which, as it were, have a foot in both modes of production: these are the small employers, who are simultaneously petty bourgeois and bourgeois; and what Wright calls 'semi-autonomous employees', who, while not owning the means of production, enjoy much more autonomy over their work tasks than do the proletariat. Such a class lies 'between' the proletariat and the petty bourgeoisie. Figure 3.1, taken from Wright (1976:27) illustrates the relative locations of the six classes that make up Wright I.

These six classes are distinguished on the basis of exploitation and domination. Relations of exploitation exist within each mode of production between those who do and do not own the means of production. Domination is measured by the amount of autonomy that can be exercised by workers and the extent to which they are involved in decision-making and the supervision of others (Marshall *et al*. 1988:24). Together these permit the identification of the six classes. So, for example, small employers are distinguished from the petty bourgeoisie by their employment of labour, and from the bourgeoisie by the small quantity of labour so employed. Managers and supervisors are distinguished from the bourgeoisie by the fact that they do not own the means of production, but, in contrast to the proletariat, they play a role in decision-making within the productive enterprise (Wright *et al*. 1982:713).[8]

About the same time that Wright launched a major 'Comparative Project on Class Structure and Class Consciousness' he began to rethink the criteria for identifying contradictory class locations. The result is a 12-class schema (Wright 1985). This dramatic leap in the number of classes occurs entirely within the propertyless middle-class sector that is the focus for all of Wright's work: 'solving the puzzle of the middle class' (Wright 1989b:306).

The major impetus for revision was Wright's dissatisfaction, and that of his critics, with the supporting role allocated to domination in his original effort. So distinctions based on domination in Wright I are replaced with exploitation in Wright II for an 'all exploitation' class map that accords better with Marxist orthodoxy. This requires a new approach to delineating exploitation relations. Exploitation now is seen to operate in contemporary societies along three dimensions: ownership of the means of production, ownership of organizational assets that permit control and coordination of technical processes of production, and ownership of skills or credentials.[9] Whereas in Wright I a manager was simultaneously in the bourgeoisie and the working class, now he or she is 'in an organization-asset exploiting class and in the working class' (Wright 1989b:306, footnote 51).

To operationalize this scheme requires survey instruments that extract considerable detail from respondents concerning employment conditions. In particular, much fine-tuning is required to measure the degree to which a respondent possesses a particular asset. A threefold distinction is made for each asset into dominant, contradictory, and subordinate class positions.

The classification process proceeds in this way. An initial distinction is drawn between those who are owners of the means of production and those who are not. Among the former the number of employees is then used to make a tripartite division between bourgeoisie (owners with 10 or more employees), small employers (with between two and 10 employees), and the petty bourgeoisie (those who have either one or no employees). These, then, are held to isolate, respectively, the dominant, contradictory, and subordinate class positions found among owners.[10]

Attention then turns to the mass of wage earners. Each employee is ranked on the dimensions of organization assets and of skills/credential assets, the two bases of exploitation available to employees. Wright developed a 'managerial location typology' that combines several variables to create the desired threefold distinction. Employees are asked questions to ascertain whether they are directly involved in making policy decisions for the organization (distinguishing, through the wording of the survey questions, between decision-making and advisory roles) and if they are supervisors with real authority over subordinates. 'Real authority' means that the person has more than one subordinate and has both 'task' and 'sanctioning' authority. Another component of the typology derives from a question asking if the employee is a manager in a formal organizational hierarchy. Managers answer affirmatively to all these questions. A supervisor responds negatively to the policy questions and manager questions, but positively to the supervisory question. Non-managers, then, give replies indicating a lack of exploitation assets to all of the questions.[11]

The second dimension applied to employees is assets in scarce skills and credentials. Three variables are again used to forge a threefold typology. Questions ascertain the person's occupational position, education, and job autonomy. The dominant class position of *Expert* consists of persons whose occupation is that of professional or manager, who possess a BA or higher degree from a third-level educational institution, and job autonomy. *Marginal skills*/credential assets are possessed by persons with occupations like school teachers, and craft workers regardless of their educational accomplishments. However, managers and technicians fall into this degree of asset exploitation only if they lack a BA, while those employees engaged in sales and clerical jobs fit the criteria only if they have a BA or higher degree and are autonomous in their work. This leaves the *uncredentialled*: those in sales and clerical occupations who lack a BA or have a BA and are 'non-autonomous'. Employees in the manual, non-craft occupations are treated as uncredentialled by definition.

The penultimate step is to combine the dimensions of organization assets and skills/credential assets to create nine possible employee classes. So the true proletariat consists of employees who are uncredentialled non-managers: they rank subordinate on both dimensions. And the final step is to add the owners of the means of production, resulting in a twelve-fold class structure. The full set of class configurations based on exploitation assets is shown in Figure 3.2. One can think of the schema as axes linking, or rather separating, the bourgeoisie from the proletariat. As one moves from the bottom right-hand corner in any direction, the overall level of exploitation suffered decreases. It is noteworthy that this massive classification effort, invoked to devise a class structure based solely on exploitation, makes virtually no difference whatsoever, when compared with Wright I, as to which persons are be classified as members of the proletariat (Pawson, 1989:285).[12]

Now 12 classes are unwieldy, whether for conducting research or exhorting the exploited to storm the barricades. Typically, Wright himself uses a sixfold structure comprising the 'self-employed' (classes 1, 2, and 3), 'credentialled managers' (classes 4 and 7), 'credentialled supervisors' (classes 5 and 8), 'credentialled employees' (classes 6 and 9), 'uncredentialled managers and supervisors' (classes 10 and 11), and 'workers' (class 12) (Marshall *et al.* 1988:38). In general, though, Wright clearly views the proliferation of classes as desirable, if unintended:

> the new class concept provided a particularly nuanced empirical map for studying the relationship between class structure and class formation . . . The proliferation of concrete structural 'locations' within this map allows for a much more subtle empirical investigation of the ways in which people within these locations become collectively organized into class formations. (Wright 1989b:307)

In short, the middle class – or segments of it, perhaps in coalition – are identified as agents of change in opposition to capital. The proletariat has lost its monopoly as the opposition to the capitalist class. The rise of the middle class can now proceed to unimagined heights.

Assets in the means of production

	Owners of means of production	Non-owners (wage labourers)		
Owns sufficient capital to hire workers and not work	1 Bourgeoisie	4 Expert manager	7 Semi-credentialled managers	10 Uncredentialled managers	+
Owns sufficient capital to hire workers but must work	2 Small employers	5 Expert supervisors	8 Semi-credentialled supervisors	11 Uncredentialled supervisors	>0
Owns sufficient capital to work for self but not to hire workers	3 Petty bourgeoisie	6 Expert non-managers	9 Semi-credentialled workers	12 Proletarians	−
		+	>0	−	Skill/credential assets

Figure 3.2 Typology of class locations in capitalist society (Source: Wright 1985: 88).

This potential is associated with other benefits that, to Wright, bring his approach to class structure more in tune with classical Marxist theory and concerns. Exploitation is now the 'organizing principle' in his class analysis, albeit indirectly, because the class map reflects *relations* to assets that generate exploitation. Such an all-exploitation approach can be reconciled with an historical materialist theory of history through the sequencing of forms of exploitation as associated with specific modes of production. The new scheme thus adds substantial breadth, being applicable to all societies – feudal, capitalist, and statist, as well as to a yet to be realized socialist variant (Wright 1989b:306–8; see also the slightly different claims for the benefits of Wright II over Wright I in Wright 1989a:27–8).

Such conceptual gains must be balanced against some methodological quibbles. Wright's measures are blunt instruments relative to the theoretical precision they are meant to implement. This is most evident in the choice of divisions along each dimension of asset exploitation. Here, as usual, Wright is perhaps his own most articulate critic:

> There are, needless to say, a host of methodological problems with these measures, particularly the measures of skill/credential assets. For this reason I have trichotomized each of the assets. The two poles of each dimension constitute positions with unambiguous relations to the asset in question. The 'intermediate' position is a combination of cases with marginal assets and cases for which the measures are ambiguous. (Wright 1989a:34)

This speaks to the reliability of Wright's classes, specifically whether other researchers with the same raw data would have made the same assignments of persons to class positions. There are also issues of validity. Do employers of 10 or more persons in fact represent the class that Wright wishes to isolate as the bourgeoisie? The main difficulty, however, is with the classes in the middle. Reliable and valid distinctions are essential here, because it is mapping the middle class that animates Wright's entire enterprise. Finally, a 12-class structure is more plausible in terms of what Weber described as 'economic classes' rather than social classes. As specific contexts, there seems little scope for processes of mediate or proximate structuration, to now borrow Giddens's terminology, to generate social classes.[13]

The Goldthorpe class schema

Unlike the Erik Olin Wright class schemata, the class categories used by John Goldthorpe and the allocation of positions to them have remained essentially unchanged since the schema's first use in the course of the Oxford Mobility Study of the 1970s (Goldthorpe and Llewellyn 1977). Nevertheless, the rationale underlying the classification has shifted somewhat. Initially, the class schema was seen to 'bring together, within the classes we distinguish, occupations whose incumbents will typically share in broadly similar *market* and *work* situations which . . . we take as the two major components of class position' (Goldthorpe *et al.* 1980/87:39). More recently, however, we read that 'The aim of the class schema is to differentiate positions within *labour markets* and *production units* or, more specifically . . . to differentiate such positions in terms of the *employment relations* that they entail' (Erikson and Gold-thorpe 1992b:37). Furthermore, this later account of the class schema is far more comprehensive and detailed than any of Goldthorpe's previous discussions of the issue.

In focusing on employment relations the first distinction made is that between employers, the self-employed and employees. Among the self-employed a sectoral distinction is made between farmers (class IVc in the schema shown in Table 3.1) and non-agricultural self-employment (class IVb). Within the group of employees classes are further defined on the basis of the employment relationship they enjoy. Here the chief distinction is between occupations that are regulated by a service relationship and those based on a labour contract. So, the Service class (classes I and II in the schema) enjoy, as their name suggests, a service relationship, while the manual classes (VI and VII) are those with a labour contract relationship with their employer. Between these two extremes lie the aptly named Intermediate classes (III and V).

Unlike the labour contract, in which the exchange of wages for effort is very specific and the worker is relatively closely super-vised, the service relationship is more long term and involves a more diffuse exchange. It is typically found in bureaucracies, or, more generally, where, by virtue of the employee's specialized knowledge or exercise of delegated authority, direct supervision is not feasible or is undesirable. 'A service relationship can thus be understood as the means through which an employing organiza-

Table 3.1 Goldthorpe class schema.

Goldthorpe class designation	Description	Employment relations
I	Higher-grade professionals, administrators and officials; managers in large industrial establishments; large proprietors	Employer or service relationship
II	Lower-grade professionals, administrators and officials; higher-grade technicians; managers in small industrial establishments; supervisors of non-manual employees	Service relationship
IIIa	Routine non-manual employees, higher-grade (administration and commerce)	Intermediate
IIIb	Routine non-manual employees, lower-grade (sales and services)	Intermediate
IVa	Small proprietors, artisans, etc., with employees	Employer
IVb	Small proprietors, artisans, etc., without employees	Self-employed
IVc	Farmers and smallholders; other self-employed workers in primary production	Employer or self-employed
V	Lower-grade technicians; supervisors of manual workers	Intermediate
VI	Skilled manual workers	Labour contract
VIIa	Semi- and unskilled manual workers (not in agriculture, etc.)	Labour contract
VIIb	Agricultural and other workers in primary production	Labour contract

tion seeks to create and sustain . . . commitment' (Erikson and Goldthorpe 1992b:42). These means include a salary and fringe benefits, and, Erikson and Goldthorpe (1992b:42) stress, 'important *prospective* elements – for example, salary increments on an established scale, assurances of security, . . . pension rights . . . and . . . well defined career opportunities'.

Within the Service class, the distinction between classes I and II and, within the Working class between classes VI and VII, is one of degree.[14] So, for example, positions in class I 'offer the fullest range of beneficial conditions associated with the service relationship' (Erikson and Goldthorpe 1992b:43) while, in class II, 'certain of these features may be attenuated'. The Intermediate class comprises class III (made up of clerical, personal service, sales and similar occupations) and class V (lower level supervisory and technical workers). These are all 'positions with associated employment relationships that would appear characteristically to take on a very mixed form' (Erikson and Goldthorpe 1992b:42).

The Goldthorpe schema also distinguishes between class IIIa (higher-grade routine non-manual workers) and IIIb (lower-grade routine non-manual workers, chiefly employed in services and sales). The latter are largely occupied by women and, when occupied by women, are clearly regulated by a labour contract, rather than a service relationship. So, in the application of the schema to women, class IIIb is treated in the same fashion as class VII. Class VII is itself divided, in this case on a sectoral basis, between semi-skilled and unskilled manual workers in agriculture (VIIb) and outside agriculture (VIIa).

The employer category is less unproblematic than it might at first seem. 'Employers', distinguished in the schema, are small proprietors with employees, placed in class IVa. This is because, nowadays, large employers are organizations, rather than individuals. A class of large employers – a *haute bourgeoisie* – does not therefore appear. Such large employers as there are are placed in class I within the service class. This, so Erikson and Goldthorpe (1992b:40–1) argue, is justified on the grounds that such individuals are usually owners of enterprises which differ from those of the petty bourgeoisie in legal, rather than substantive, terms. They are separated from the petty bourgeoisie in the schema because, being involved in the management of their enterprises, they have more in common with the salaried managers who are also placed in class I.

In total, then, this yields a class schema which, starting from the threefold distinction of employers, the self-employed and employees, has 11 classes, as shown in Table 3.1 which reports the class designation (in Roman numerals and letters), its description, and the nature of the employment relations characterizing the occupational positions within the class.

Given these criteria for defining classes, how are individuals allocated to them? Compared with the tortuous procedures required by the Wright II schema, the method is disarmingly straightforward. When applied to the data for England and Wales individuals are allocated to one of the 549 occupational categories defined by the British Office of Population Censuses and Surveys (OPCS). They are also assigned to one of nine OPCS employment status categories, which distinguish, *inter alia*, between employees, employers, and the self-employed, and, for those in supervisory positions, the number of people supervised. Classes are operationalized as aggregates based on these two criteria: in other words, each possible combination of occupation and employment status is assigned to a particular class, and individuals are thus allocated according to this simple algorithm. A similar procedure was followed in the CASMIN project; here, however, different algorithms were applied to different nations (Erikson and Goldthorpe 1992b:50–1; Goldthorpe 1990:435, footnote 4). This follows, of course, given that first, the aim of the schema is to group occupational title/employment status combinations on the basis of their employment relations, and second, that the employment relationships enjoyed by given combinations may differ cross-nationally (albeit to a limited extent).

Goldthorpe's class schema provides no information about 'elite' groups at the apex of the class structure.[15] Goldthorpe accepts that such groups may 'have some special significance for the sociological purposes to which the results of the (mobility) inquiry are put' (Goldthorpe *et al.* 1980/87:286, parentheses added) but points out that the rarity of members of such groups in the population means that any sample survey will contain very few of them. On this basis it could well be argued that the schema's categories are inadequate to capture a sociologically significant distinction, and, indeed, that the problem is compounded by placing members of the *haute bourgeoisie* in class I alongside salaried managers. This would be problematic if Goldthorpe (like Runciman 1990 or like Wright and other neo-Marxists) was seeking to provide a definitive 'class map' of a society. But, as we discuss below, this is emphatically not Goldthorpe's purpose; rather, his class schema is an *instrument de travail* (Erikson and Goldthorpe 1992b:46). In this sense it is to be judged according to how well it serves the purpose of the particular analysis in which it is applied. Goldthorpe argues that national mobility studies treat mobility and class structure in a 'broad-brush way' (Goldthorpe *et al.* 1980/87:287). For this purpose the class schema so defined is, presumably, considered adequate, but Goldthorpe accepts that more specialized studies will be needed to capture mobility patterns relating to elite groupings.

A more trenchant criticism concerns the neglect of women in class analysis. This is not simply a question of their absence from Goldthorpe's (and others') mobility studies, but the fact that the class schema itself is not considered adequate to capture the class position of women in paid employment outside the home (Heath and Britten 1984; Murgatroyd 1984; Dale *et al.* 1985). It was in response to such criticisms that Goldthorpe made the distinction between classes IIIa and IIIb to which we referred. Feminist critics have not been mollified, however. In particular, when women are classified according to the schema, they are found to be heavily concentrated in classes II, III, and VIIa.[16] While this reflects the gendered nature of the occupational structure, in which women are clustered in lower grade jobs (both manual and non-manual), it has been argued that this obscures important distinctions between women at work (Martin and Wallace 1984) which an adequate class schema should identify. However, as Marshall *et al.* (1994) point out, the kinds of distinctions that critics make are typically to do with whether or not a woman has children, her level of educational attainment, and aspects of lifestyle. Many of these might be more appropriately considered to be related to the woman's position within the stages of the family cycle rather than to class.[17]

Comparing classes: Goldthorpe and Wright

Students of stratification differ not only in their image of class structure, as shown in the preceding chapter, but also in the time and care that they devote to constructing and justifying class categories. Contemporary neo-Marxists often regard the mapping of the current class structure of the advanced societies as the royal road to the essence of capitalism and thus to the potential for its demise or at least its domestication. Erik Olin Wright has perhaps been the most arduous in refining definitions of classes, seeking rigour where Marx was unsystematic and also taking into account the changing face of the capitalist system itself. Such effort is justified because precise delineation of class structure is an essential precondition to serious analysis, meriting decades of spadework in order to perfect it.[18] Class structure, once stripped bare, encapsulates the dynamics and contradictions of an epoch. To understand class structure is to understand, and anticipate, large-scale change processes and, specifically, to identify the class that will uproot the system of exploitation: 'Current debates about the boundaries of classes are important for they relate to the project of locating the class most likely to carry out this historical charge' (McNall *et al.* 1991:12).

Goldthorpe's approach is quite different. Erikson and Goldthorpe (1992b:46) 'wish to emphasize that the schema we have presented is to be regarded not as an attempt at providing a definitive "map" of the class structures of individual societies but essentially as an *instrument de travail.*' One index of this is the nominalism they display in regard to the number of classes to be distinguished. In his own work and that with Erikson, Goldthorpe never, in fact, uses the full 11-category version of his class schema. In *The Constant Flux* analyses are undertaken on seven-, five-, and three-class versions of the scheme, obtained through amalgamating certain of the original classes. Thus, in reply to a query such as Runciman's (1990) as to how many classes exist in a given social formation, Erikson and Goldthorpe (1992b:46, footnote 18) reply 'As many as it proves empirically useful to distinguish for the analytical purposes in hand'.

The logic of their argument, cast in the terms we have been using, is that, for some sets of actions, differences in social power might arise only between, say, a small number of large groups, while for other sets of actions resources and constraints might be much more finely distributed. The important thing, however, is that if we are to argue that we are dealing with the same basis of stratification in both cases then we must define the strata (in this case classes) using the same criteria (ownership and employment relationships) albeit with different cut-off points.

A further point of disagreement between the Wright and Goldthorpe schemata concerns whether or not classes are in an exploitative relationship, one to another. Goldthorpe (Goldthorpe and Marshall 1992:383) explicitly rejects this, whereas Wright's schema is based on the concept of exploitation. For neo-Marxists the exploitative and (potentially) antagonistic relationship between classes provides the key to the evolution of society – thus the effort devoted to identifying that class which will act as history's agent. That line of reasoning, even as heroically pursued by Wright (1978 and subsequently), is, in our view, one of social science's culs-de-sac. The intellectual sterility of efforts to resuscitate the notion of a proletariat that can stand as a class-for-itself or to find a contemporary functional equivalent seems self-evident (see Newby *et al.* 1985:91–2).

A more modest rationale suffices to make class structure a key concept for the sociological imagination. Classes are the most important context within which resources are allocated and preferences are exercised (see Pawson 1989:216). The prevailing class structure strongly affects variation in the quality of life and in political consciousness within a society. Of course, class explains only a portion of this variance (see Marshall *et al.* 1988), and the explanatory power of class in these respects differs among societies (e.g. Holtmann and Strasser 1990). Class structure also shapes the relationship between the state and civil society, and indeed between the state and the capitalist enterprise. The irritants underlying social conflict today are increasingly complex and 'opaque' and conflict is predominantly over distributional issues and policies (again, see Newby *et al.* 1985:92–3; also Scase 1992). The notion that classes must be inherently entities in conflict with one another is no longer sustainable.

Within this more modest rationale for class analysis, both Wright and Goldthorpe provide a foundation for empirical inquiry. Each offers a model in which class structure is the most important basis for the distribution of social power: 'Wright's basic thesis is that the class structure constitutes the central mechanism by which various sets of resources are appropriated and distributed, therefore determining the underlying capacities to act of various social actors' (Pawson 1989:189). This parallels the thesis put forward by Erikson and Goldthorpe (1992b:236). Class position determines 'experiences of affluence or hardship, of economic security or insecurity, of prospects of continuing material advance, or of unyielding material constraints'.

We are thus faced with two alternative approaches to class structure that meet our criteria for class analysis. Distinctions according to the nature of the labour contract are secondary to Wright; conversely, Erikson and Goldthorpe (1992b:47, footnote 19, parentheses added) do not 'find the theoretical basis of either of these (Wright I and II) sociologically convincing'. One basis for choosing which to adopt is a comparison of the relative power of each schema for predicting inequalities in life chances, class consciousness and preferences, and forms of behaviour such as voting that might reasonably be supposed to be largely class determined. Marshall *et al.* (1988, particularly chapters 3, 6, 7, 8 and 9) arranged such a contest. They tested the explanatory power of the Goldthorpe and Wright I schemata on a number of outcome measures, including class mobility, voting intentions, attitudes towards distributional justice, and an index of class consciousness. In all cases they found that the Goldthorpe schema emerged as the more powerful predictor. In other words, across their sample members, variation in these outcome measures was structured more clearly according to the class categories derived from the Goldthorpe schema than from those of Wright I. Such a competition can be conclusive from the vantage point of those who have a clear theoretical purpose for which the classification is to be employed. In most of what follows we therefore adhere to the Goldthorpe approach to class analysis. The next chapter, however, extends the comparison between Wright and Goldthorpe through an examination of the class structures of nine societies.

Notes

1. The most notable examples include the International Class Structure and Class Consciousness project, using the Wright schemata, and the CASMIN (Comparative Analysis of Social Mobility in Industrial Nations) project, employing the Goldthorpe class schema. The latter analyzed data from the early 1970s relating to nine European nations (if we count Northern Ireland and Scotland as nations) plus Australia, Japan, and the United States. The results of the analysis form the basis of Erikson and Goldthorpe (1992b).
2. Although this change has made little difference in practice to the way in which occupations are classified (Brewer 1986).

3. Of course, patterns of mobility between positions potentially affect the resiliency of class boundaries and the likelihood that positions with similar economic characteristics also share common social attributes (a tenet of both Marxist and neo-Weberian approaches to stratification, and perhaps of contemporary class theory – see Erikson and Goldthorpe 1992b:29, footnote 1). Runciman (1990:393, footnote 2) argues that the explanatory power of class position remains unaffected even if the occupants of positions change very rapidly.

4. Formally, Erikson distinguishes market situation, which is a characteristic of families, roughly captured in the idea of their collective life chances, from work situation, which concerns the location of an individual's occupation within systems of authority and control. However, as others have noted, market situation depends to a great extent on work situation (Abercrombie and Urry 1983). Erikson's criteria of dominance, then, rank work situations on the basis of their impact on market situation.

5. As might be expected, these issues take us into controversial terrain. There is much debate as to whether or not it should be the individual, rather than the family, which is to be considered the fundamental unit of class composition. These are issues we look at it in more detail in Chapter 7.

6. Interestingly, Wright is once again an exception: neither of his schemata draw this sectoral distinction.

7. This is based on the current class of men in the early 1970s as reported in surveys of social mobility in 12 countries (the CASMIN data analyzed by Erikson and Goldthorpe 1992b). The importance of the sectoral distinction for studies of comparative mobility is indexed by the variability across countries in the proportion of respondents whose class of origin is agricultural: farmers account for between 5 and 53 per cent of the class of origin and agricultural labourers for between 3 and 22 per cent.

8. Wright made a number of finer distinctions within certain of his six class categories. The one which will be relevant to our discussion in Chapter 4 is that between members of the class of top executives, managers and supervisors. Here Wright distinguishes three 'sub classes' – managers, advisory managers, and supervisors – on the basis of the authority they possess.

9. To be concrete, we quote two examples, *the* principal examples, according to Wright (1989b:306): 'managers (who are capitalistically exploited but organization exploiters) and experts (who are capitalistically exploited but skill/credential exploiters)'.

10. Wright's intention was to restrict the petty bourgeoisie to its standard composition of 'own account' workers without paid employees.

However, ambiguity in the relevant survey question leaves open the possibility that some, unknown, proportion of self-employed respondents regarded themselves as being the employee of their business (see Wright 1985:150). Wright thus had to choose whether to place all respondents with one employee as being either subordinate or contradictory in terms of their property ownership. He chose the former with the associated risk of overstating the size of the class of those with the least exploitation assets.

11. Wright (1985:150) notes that reference was made to a variety of other criteria to cope with cases in which the responses seemed contradictory, as when someone claims a policy role in the organization but no supervisory authority over subordinates.

12. The complex facets of Wright's classification are given a lively and clear rendition by Pawson (1989:308–18), who uses Wright's questionnaire to illustrate the argument that an interview is an exercise in data construction rather than merely data collection. More generally, Pawson (1989) draws extensively upon the class analysis of both Goldthorpe and Wright to explain the logic of 'generative models' in the social sciences.

13. See Marshall *et al.* (1988:39–43) for a critique grounded in the experience of implementing Wright's questionnaire and classification instructions using British data.

14. Erikson and Goldthorpe (1992b:43, footnote 16) are adamant that it is not the manual nature of these occupations that leads to them being classed together: the criterion used is their shared labour contract relationship. It is simply an empirical fact that the manual/non-manual distinction corresponds quite closely to that between a labour contract and a service relationship.

15. Though the term 'apex' suggests a hierarchical notion of class structure, Goldthorpe has been at pains to stress that the schema is explicitly *non*-hierarchical.

16. See, for example, Marshall *et al.* 1988:74, Table 4.6.

17. In recent years the 'feminist' critique of Goldthorpe's approach to class analysis has been vigorously pursued (see Dex 1990). We postpone further discussion of this to Chapter 7.

18. Other less empirically minded neo-Marxists are impatient with Wright's obsession with getting the statistical portrait of the class structure correct. And, despite the investment in depicting the American class structure (e.g. Wright *et al.* 1982 and Wright and Martin 1987), Wright's defensiveness is evident: 'Ultimately, we are not so much interested in studying class structures simply for their own sake, but because we feel class is a systematic determinant of macro- and micro-social outcomes' (Wright *et al.* 1982:725).

Additionally, however, Wright's flexibility offends the more orthodox. Wright (1989b:276) appears to endorse Erikson and Goldthorpe's view (cited later in this chapter) that class boundaries should be constructed to fit one's analytical purpose: 'The specific class structure concept that one adopts will depend upon the kind of question one is asking', although Wright adds the proviso that the alternative concepts must all belong to 'a unitary conceptual logic' that he would argue Weberian theorists lack.

CHAPTER 4

CLASS STRUCTURE IN ADVANCED SOCIETIES: PATTERNS AND VARIATIONS

Class structure

We turn here from abstract debate about the nature of social classes and the mechanics of class assignment to the more concrete question of what class structures look like in contemporary society. In doing so, this chapter tries to advance our argument along two main lines. One is to translate the ideas of theorists into structures that we can recognize as part of our social landscapes. The second is to get a sense of which aspects of class are generic to either capitalism or to phases of capitalist development and which are susceptible to local (regional or national) influences. With this accomplished we can more readily place the idea of class within an analytical framework that embraces both time and space.

Our examination of class structure involves three steps. The first step is to look at the class structures of nine countries through the lenses of both Weberian and Marxist theorists. The second step is to consider processes of change that may currently be reshaping the class structures that we have described. And the third step is to assess what we have learned.

In preparation, we briefly indicate our own views on why an examination of specific class structures is an important component of any understanding of social stratification. We will be applying theories of social class to contemporary societies in order to locate the basic structures within which differences in social power reside. So we ask such questions as: How many classes are there? What is the essence that gives coherence to a class? What proportion of the population belongs to particular classes? How formidable are the boundaries that separate those classes?

These are essentially descriptive questions, uncovering the main lines of inequalities that stratify the societies in which we live. The connection to theory, however, is direct and vigorous: 'Sociological theories inevitably take the form of specifying the groups into which society is divided, identifying the properties which differentiate those groups and explaining why these properties are apportioned in different degrees' (Pawson 1989:188). We argue that, for several purposes, social classes are the most fundamental of the groups constituting contemporary society.

For this reason, identifying class structures should be more than an exercise in taxonomy.[1] Social classes are so important to understanding contemporary societies that their description inevitably raises questions concerning the very nature of capitalist society. A reasonable starting point for our purposes is to ask what the class structures of advanced capitalist societies have in common, and whether such commonality as we find can be associated with features of 'late' or 'advanced capitalism'. This leads to the questions of where class structures diverge, and whether those divergences are vestiges of their national histories, of diversity in placement within the world-system, or of socio-political idiosyncrasies. A contrast between the nations comprising capitalist Europe and the (formerly) state socialist nations of Eastern Europe offers a particularly helpful tool in answering such questions, as does a contrast between Europe and the younger class structures of North America and Japan.

Nine class structures in a 'Golden Age'

The period 1945–73 was a 'Golden Age' of capitalism, three decades of sustained and substantial economic growth across Western Europe, North America, the Antipodes, and Southeast Asia (see Bairoch 1981; Maddison 1982).[2] We offer two views of class structure during that era. One is based on the perspective of Erik Olin Wright: specifically, eight classes derived from the Wright I classification. This entails a threefold distinction among the 'owners' of property into the bourgeoisie, small employers, and petty bourgeoisie; three middle classes comprised of managers, advisory managers, and supervisors; a class of semi-autonomous wage earners, and, finally, the proletariat. Small employers, managers, and semi-autonomous workers all represent 'contradictory' class locations, whose members belong simultaneously to two classes (e.g. as employees, managers are exploited by capital, but they dominate other employees through the authority structure of capitalist enterprises).[3]

The second class structure is a sevenfold categorization developed by Goldthorpe and his colleagues for research on comparative social mobility (Erikson and Goldthorpe 1992b). Note that both depictions of the class structure are based on males in the workforce, but that while Erikson and Goldthorpe explicitly isolate the situation of farmers in the class structure, Wright does not.

The class structures of a small number of countries cannot be more than illustrative. Here, the United States and Japan represent the centre of the new world system; Britain, France, and Germany the old; Ireland and Sweden can represent the periphery of the centre in, respectively, relative penury and prosperity; Australia and Hungary represent distinctive instances, offering, respectively, glimpses of an emergent capitalist economy and of a command economy. All are countries with traditions of class analysis and, consequently, for which data are available to us for secondary analysis.[4]

Although 'class divisions cannot be drawn like lines on a map', as Giddens admonishes (1973:273), the categories imposed on the nine countries included in Table 4.1 can claim to be theoretically derived and to include those class boundaries that are currently the most disputed terrain within the field of stratification.

Through the lens ground by Erikson and Goldthorpe, three classes are seen to dominate (at least in proportionate numbers) the class structure of all nine countries: the Service Class, Skilled Workers, and Non-Skilled Workers. There is broad similarity in the proportion of positions that each of these classes represents. The service class is most substantial, at least numerically, in the United States and Australia; it has the least presence in Ireland and Hungary. Skilled workers are most prominent in England and Sweden, and also in Hungary where they account for about one-third of class positions. Non-skilled workers are prevalent in Hungary and the United States and more prevalent than skilled

Table 4.1 The class structures of nine advanced societies.

(a) Goldthorpe's classes	Sweden %	Germany %	France %	England %	Ireland %	Hungary %	United States %	Australia %	Japan %
Service class	24	28	21	25	14	15	28	27	24
Routine non-manual	8	5	10	9	9	7	11	8	16
Petty bourgeoisie	8	7	10	8	8	2	7	12	13
Farmers	5	4	11	2	22	1	3	7	10
Skilled workers	30	37	24	33	20	31	24	27	20
Non-skilled workers	22	18	21	22	21	30	26	16	14
Agricultural labourers	2	1	3	2	7	14	1	2	3
Total	**100**	**100**	**100**	**100**	**100**	**100**	**100**	**100**	**100**
Year of reference	1974	1976–8	1970	1972	1973–4	1973	1973	1973–4	1975

(b) **Wright's classes**	Sweden %	Germany %	France %	England %	Ireland %	Hungary %	United States %	Australia %	Japan %
Bourgeoisie	1	1		3			3	5	
Small employer	7	7		7			7		
Petty bourgeoisie	7	3		7			6	11	
Managers	16	9		15			16	15	
Advisory managers	4	0.5		6			5	15	
Supervisors	7	12		10			14	8	
Semi-autonomous wage-earners	15	19		9			9	7	
Proletariat	43	50		43			40	39	
Total	**100**	**100**		**100**			**100**	**100**	
Year of reference	1980	1979		1984			1980	1979	

Source: Goldthorpe classes: Sweden, Germany, England, Ireland, Hungary (Erikson and Goldthorpe 1992b:193); United States and Australia (Erikson and Goldthorpe 1992b:328); Japan (Erikson and Goldthorpe 1992b:353). Wright classes: Holtmann and Strasser 1990:12. A Wright-inspired class structure is not currently available for Hungary, France, Ireland, or Japan, and it is not possible to separate the bourgeoisie from small employers in the Australian class structure. Rounding error leads to some totals exceeding 100 per cent.

workers in both the United States and in Ireland. Configurations of class structure do differ.

Through the neo-Marxist lens supplied by Wright we find a proletariat that constitutes about 40 per cent of class positions in all five countries. Positions occupied by managers and advisory managers tend to account for one-fifth of the male workforce, with the exception of Germany where the proportion is one-tenth (due to the virtual absence of advisory managerial positions), and Australia, where nearly one-third of the male workforce consists of managerial employees. Overall, the class structures of Sweden, France, England, and the United States are similar. Differences are noteworthy only for the petty bourgeoisie (which is disproportionately large in Australia) and semi-autonomous wage-earners (a position most prevalent in Sweden). Germany, however, has a class structure weighted towards the proletariat, semi-autonomous wage-earners, and supervisors. Combined, those three classes account for nearly 80 per cent of the male German workforce. The same three class positions represent some 55 per cent of the Australian workforce.

One way of looking at this map is in terms of the proportionate share of contradictory class positions, and whether those positions are essentially middle class or working class. Germany, and to a lesser extent Sweden, are the only countries with large concentrations of working-class employees in a contradictory location; for the most part, however, contradictions occur within the middle class, particularly if one extends that designation to include small employers.

What implications follow from these two sets of class maps? First, the theoretical orientation underlying a class map is clearly evident in the proportion of the populations that are allocated to various classes. This is true despite the coincidence of manual/non-manual, supervisory/non-supervisory, large proprietor and small proprietor distinctions in the class schemes of both Wright and Goldthorpe. So, although much of the sharpness is gone from the intellectual content, if not the rhetoric, of what divides neo-Marxists from neo-Weberians in the field of stratification, they do see rather different class structures. Two differences are fundamental. First, neo-Marxists find a large working class/proletariat. Erik Olin Wright versions I and II place one-half of the workforce in an undifferentiated 'proletariat' class location in the advanced societies if both females and males are included, and about 40 per cent based on males alone (Holtmann and Strasser 1990:12). A more orthodox Marxist definition of class places two-thirds of the workforce in the 'working class' (Szymanski 1983:112).[5]

Second, advanced capitalism is only weakly associated with a specific pattern by which classes account for various shares of the working population. Class maps do not neatly fall into categories of 'core' and 'periphery' (see Holtmann and Strasser 1990) or even European and non-European (Haller 1990). Similarities among countries are more striking when the comparison is based on Wright's class categories. Using the Goldthorpe schema strong differences are present in the proportion of the workforce that is in the skilled worker class, which ranges from 20 per cent (Japan) to 37 per cent (Germany). One consequence is that the Goldthorpe and Wright schemes paint very different portraits of the distribution of credentials and skills in the class structure. According to Wright, Germany is atypical in the size of its proletariat; to Goldthorpe, Germany stands out for the unusually high level of skill among its workers.

The position of the 'service class' is another case in point. By the 1970s, a broadly similar way of organizing large-scale enterprises can be found in the capitalist core and beyond:

> managers with little or no equity in the enterprises administered made the decisions about present production and distribution and the allocation of resources for future production and distribution . . . Nevertheless, variations within this new brand of capitalism are still significant . . . reflecting the different routes by which the leading sectors of each economy reached managerial capitalism. (Chandler 1984/92:156)[6]

Third, claims that are made for the exceptionalism of the United States, Australia, and Japan are not strongly supported, although only a Goldthorpe-based class map is available for the latter country. The commonality found in the core capitalist countries is less pronounced in a class structure mapped according to Goldthorpe's perspective, but is evident nonetheless. This leaves open the question of whether the use of a small number of categories that combine economic sector with other criteria is not concealing important points of variation within countries. The available class maps suggest the importance of looking at differences *within* the working class and the middle classes.

Historical processes and class structures

Class structures of Western industrial societies are variations on a common theme. The theme is capitalism and the variations tend to be specific to nation-states. We can identify some processes of change within the capitalist system that are likely over coming decades to alter the size of various classes and perhaps level the boundaries between some. Four are of particular interest: (1) the shifting fortunes of the small enterprise and small entrepreneur – the independent petty bourgeoisie; (2) changes in the accumulation and control of capital; and (3) in the nature of the state sector, and (4) the existence of an excluded sector or underclass – positions for non-participation in the capitalist economy.[7] We examine these trends in turn.

The fate of the petty bourgeoisie

Claims that the middle class is rising and the family disintegrating are two mainstays of social commentary in the modern era.[8] Whatever the current state of the family, the prosperity of the middle class is critical to understanding the shape of change in the class structure. One segment of the middle class in particular seems to be thriving, confounding predictions of its demise: that of the small proprietor. Because the gradual demise of the petty bourgeoisie constitutes Marx's chief claim to prescience about the course of capitalist development during this century, such a reversal is of considerable potential significance for class structure. In current usage, the petty bourgeoisie includes both the artisan who neither hires nor sells labour power (the 'pure' petty bourgeoisie) and small employers, with small covering most enterprises that have individuals or families as their majority owners.[9]

What exactly has changed? Since the 1970s the number of non-agricultural proprietor positions has increased across Western Europe, particularly in Belgium, Ireland, Italy, and the United Kingdom (Steinmetz and Wright 1989). A similar pattern can be identified in the United States.[10] This reverses a century-long trend of declining numbers.

The apparent reversal of fortune experienced by the petty bourgeoisie is sufficiently broadly based to be regarded as a correlate of macroeconomic conditions that are typical of 'late' capitalism. This should translate into a visible shift in class structure. But which macroeconomic conditions are responsible? One view is that post-golden age capitalism is weighted in favour of small firms using flexible forms of production. Such firms are better situated to accommodate the fluctuating or low levels of demand that have become characteristic of the market than are firms which continue to rely on mass production (Steinmetz and Wright 1989:987). This suggests that an expanding and resilient independent proprietorial class will be an important component of the class structure. Small in the scale of operations and small in the overall scheme of capitalist production, the strengthening of the petty bourgeoisie nevertheless broadens the class structure.

A very different scenario flows from an assumption that the operative macroeconomic change is one of proletarianization. Self-employment is increasing, under this scenario, because it permits large firms to substitute high-wage (and benefit) employees with cheaper contract and freelance workers (Linder and Houghton 1990; Dale 1986). This less benign and perhaps more transient characterization of the trend towards rising self-employment is made concrete by claims that one-third of the rise in the petty bourgeoisie that Steinmetz and Wright (1989) observe in the United States is accounted for by positions as maids, janitors, hairdressers, and child-care workers (Linder and Houghton 1990:730–1). Growing self-employment in such economic pursuits is more likely to expand the ranks of the lumpen proletariat than that of even a quasi-independent middle class (Dale 1986).[11]

It thus remains to be seen whether the demographic vitality of the small proprietor class creates a class that is advantaged or disadvantaged in terms of its associated life chances. The imprint on the class structure of that class's expansion, however, is likely to be considerable for the foreseeable future.

Accumulation and control of capital

The sudden resurgence of the 'independent' middle class is associated with changes to capitalist accumulation and control that fall under the general label of post-modern. If the mass assembly production line is emblematic of the modern, 'flexible production' characterizes the post-modern.

Flexible accumulation embraces small-scale production and subcontracting (the latter underlying, in part, the sudden growth of the self-employed), as well as truly global markets. With this, capitalism, it is argued, has entered a new phase:

> the tension that has always prevailed within capitalism between monopoly and competition, between centralization and decentralization of economic power, is being worked out in fundamentally new ways . . . capitalism is becoming ever more tightly organized through dispersal, geographical mobility, and flexible responses in labour markets, labour processes, and consumer markets, all accompanied by hefty doses of institutional, product, and technological innovation. (Harvey 1989:159)

To some, this supplants the era of 'managerial capitalism' dominated by large enterprises and the associated cadre of salaried managers who make the key decisions on the deployment of capital.

One effect is to spawn a resurgent small employer sector and thus bolster the demographic significance of the petty bourgeoisie. At the same time, the trend has been for small and medium-size enterprises to become increasingly constrained by the decisions and strategies of large-scale corporations and financial markets. The implications for manual and non-manual labour tend to be portrayed rather starkly – and very differently. The most contested terrain is the likely fate of the routine non-manual class. Will it be 'degraded' and deskilled until it is clearly merged with non-skilled workers? Or, to continue using Goldthorpe's class labels, will new forms of capital accumulation and control expand the ranks, and improve the material and working conditions, of the service class? At this juncture neither trend is supported by strong evidence, but it is clear that capitalism in its post-modern manifestation does not weaken the boundaries constituting the class structure (Marshall *et al.* 1988:269–74).

The state sector

The distribution of positions within the class structure is shaped by state policies in taxation, job creation, and job training that affect the viability of various forms of wage- and self-employment. A more direct influence stems from the role of the state as an employer. The state is a significant employer in most industrial societies, capitalist and state socialist alike. 'In most major Western nations, the period since 1951 has seen a doubling in public employment as a proportion of the workforce' (Rose 1985:10). Growth in public sector employment slowed in the late 1980s and subsequently stalled. Public employment accounts for between a fourth and a third of the workforce in Britain, France, Germany, and Italy; even in the United States 18 per cent of the workforce is employed by the state (Rose 1985:11).

A substantial proportion of that public employment is devoted to welfare state programmes: health care, education, and income support. However, countries differ in the degree to which such activities are undertaken within the public or the private sectors. Virtually all (90 per cent or more) of positions associated with welfare state activities are part of the public sector in the Scandinavian countries. This contrasts with the 45 per cent of such positions that fall within the public sectors of the United States and Canada. The European core countries (e.g. Britain, France, and Germany) fall midway between the Scandinavian and North American patterns (Esping-Andersen 1990:158).

The growth of the public sector was but one feature of the welfare state expansion that accompanied the golden age of capitalist development. Prosperity in the Western democracies, and the tax revenues that it generated, certainly facilitated state expansion. However, that very prosperity was in part a product of sophisticated state strategies that fostered a context of industrial peace and cooperation between capital and labour. Welfare state institutions and policies are integral features of advanced capitalism, with the state both counteracting the negative consequences of capitalist markets on classes and blunting conflict between economic interests (Esping-Andersen 1990; Castles 1988). Indeed, the varieties of forms taken by welfare state institutions left their imprints on the nine class structures just examined.

As prosperity gave way to recession and to periodic jobless recoveries, the class structure became susceptible to fundamental change. Policies in income maintenance, education, employment creation, and tariff protection all underpin the class structure of advanced capitalist societies. A parallel set of institutions and policies once supported the class structures of Eastern Europe. In both East and West, the welfare state foundation has shifted from beneath the class structure. One key consequence is that class structures have contracted insofar as they are conceived as being constructed out of positions for economic participation. Classes have, to varying degrees – relative to one another and in different countries – lost positions to the class of those who are dependent on state transfer payments for an income. Such positions are conventionally omitted from class analysis. The apparent end of capitalism's golden age raises the question of whether the status of 'unemployed' is sufficiently stable to merit designation as a class. It is to that question that we now turn.

The underclass

A persistent theme in class analysis is the existence of an excluded sector or an underclass. Such a class consists of positions that are sufficiently detached from production and the market as to either not appear in official statistics at all or to appear in a manner that makes it difficult to incorporate into the types of class categories being used here. We can think of 'positions' and of a 'class' in this instance primarily in relation to dependence on state transfer payments as an income source.[12]

We have examined nine class structures at the culmination of the golden age of capitalism. In such a period of low unemployment, an underclass seemed a marginal phenomenon, one that was most pronounced in the United States rather than endemic to late capitalism. Indeed, the underclass label makes its first appearance in writings by social scientists concerned with distinctive features of American capitalism, subsequently being embraced by the American mass media (Katz 1993). In particular, the underclass in the 1970s refers to the point of intersection between ethnicity and class, where 'status group membership itself becomes a form of market capacity' (Giddens 1973:112):

> Where ethnic differences serve as a 'disqualifying' market capacity, such that those in the category in question are heavily concentrated among the lowest-paid occupations, or are chronically unemployed or semi-employed, we may speak of the existence of an *under*class. (Giddens, 1973:112)[13]

In the 1990s, the spectre of long-term unemployment is a more substantial challenge for class analysis. A large number of positions exist that do not offer a realistic point of entry into the labour market. Instead, a segment of the adult population occupy positions on a trajectory that goes from unemployment to retirement; in other words, from one to another, slightly more remunerative, form of transfer payment from the state.

Positions in the class structure traditionally refer to persons who are in gainful employment, whether as employees or as proprietors. The unemployed are often allocated to a class on the basis of their last job. This is Goldthorpe's procedure, although he has also treated the unemployed as a distinct class in some analyses of mobility.[14] The assumption, presumably, is that when the person re-enters the workforce they will occupy a position similar to that which they last held and that in any event the class effects associated with prior positions are extraordinarily durable. Other researchers do not assign survey respondents who have been unemployed for more than a year to a class category. The theoretical justification is that we lack current information on market and work situations (Marshall *et al.* 1988, Chapter 4). A practical reason is that some surveys, including the one used by Marshall and his colleagues, simply do not ask the long-term unemployed those questions relating to work circumstances.

Whatever the rationale for past practice, it seems incongruous in the 1990s. At current rates of long-term unemployment, and given the grim prospects for future employment faced by many in that situation, it seems unlikely that the class structure in the 1990s can be drawn without denoting the distinctive position of the long-term unemployed. Szymanski (1983:95) estimates that 8 per cent of the adult population of the United States falls within the 'excluded sector'. Runciman (1990:388) estimates that the underclass represents 5 per cent of the British population, having declined from 10 per cent in the Edwardian period. Both estimates seem low for the advanced societies in the 1990s.

Whatever the number of the long-term unemployed, their presence is a challenge to class analysis. It is unsatisfactory to define these locations as being outside of the class structure. The challenge is not limited to practicalities of survey design and analysis (see Marshall *et al.* 1988). Some argue that in late welfare-capitalism job assets become central to mapping the class structure and understanding the implicit dynamics for change: indeed, one Marxist class analyst, moving at a tangent from Wright's (1985) explication, argues that job assets have become 'even more important than the standard division between capitalists and workers in those capitalist societies in which the welfare state is most developed' (Van Parijs 1989:241).

Conclusion: So what is a class?

What is a class structure? Based on the empirical examination offered in this chapter we conclude that a class consists of locations for market participation that are broadly similar. The capacities possessed by those in a particular class are roughly equivalent, not identical. It follows that their interests, resources, preferences, allegiances, and other characteristics are likely to have sufficient in common to make the variation *within* the class less than the variation *between* that class and other classes. This is of a piece with a view of the world in which class position is an independent variable – in our view, the most important such predictor – in most sociological problems but of which class membership can explain only a part of the variance. In this respect, we have an obvious difficulty accepting the class map offered by Erik Olin Wright. Too few distinctions are made within the working class to capture the important differences in resources and interests that are present. With one-half of the population stranded in an undifferentiated proletariat, Wright's scheme is simply not very useful for our purpose.

Economic locations or positions that are sufficiently distinct to have a plausible claim to being social classes are the building blocks of a class structure. Class structure is not formed out of a static set of positions, however; rather, classes include 'career-like trajectories through sets of positions' (Goldthorpe as described in Marshall *et al.* 1988:83). To describe a class structure, then, one needs some criteria for deciding when sufficient commonality exists and also some boundary lines to say unambiguously to which class a particular family or individual belongs. Thus prepared, one can hazard an opinion as to how many classes are present in a particular society or, more ambitiously, in a particular type of society through comparative analysis.

The class structures of nine countries, when viewed comparatively, suggest that the nation-state is very much the conduit for capitalist development. It is certainly the case that a broad generic pattern fits all nine countries and, further, that their class structures are not usefully characterized as bipolar. Rather, there are at least three basic boundaries in the class structure, dividing the service class, the working class, and an intermediate class of routine non-manual workers, technicians, and the petty bourgeoisie. But individual countries display distinctive class structures that are congruent with their histories, roles in the global economy, and welfare state policies.

Classes are formed by the operations of the capitalist market. And as the capitalist market varies geographically or changes over time, so, after a lag and with idiosyncrasies, will the class structure (Newby *et al.* 1985:92-3). The class boundaries that we draw do matter. This is particularly the case for the treatment afforded the working class:

> If as Marshall (1988:105) has recently claimed, the protracted debate among sociologists of rival schools about the nature of working-class consciousness is 'grinding to a confused and untimely halt', it is partly, at least, because of their failure to agree on the answer to the 'boundary question' – that is, the criteria by which the working class is identified and located within the class structure of British society as a whole. Those for whom the working class embraces salaried employees have naturally expected the latter to behave like proletarians and have been puzzled to explain why they don't, just as those for whom the middle class embraces affluent manual workers have naturally expected the latter to behave like bourgeois. (Runciman 1990:302)

On balance, when class maps are drawn for specific countries, the class categories provided by Erikson and Goldthorpe seem more telling than those made available by neo-Marxist class theorists. Their classes capture the important variations in social power derived from the economy without creating an unwieldy number of classes.

Class maps are merely the starting point for inquiry. That roughly similar proportions of the workforce fall within the class structures of a diverse range of countries does not really tell us anything about the extent of class structuration:

> The problem of the existence of distinct class 'boundaries', there-
> fore, is not one which can be settled *in abstracto*: one of the specific
> aims of class analysis in relation to empirical societies must
> necessarily be that of determining how strongly, in any given case,
> the 'class principle' has become established. (Giddens 1973:110)

So it remains to be seen whether and to what degree positions associated with a particular class generate roughly similar life chances. In other words, are the standards of living enjoyed by skilled workers similar across countries? Or, given the range of wealth found in the nine countries we have considered, are the relativities between classes in their typical life chances similar?

Another unresolved issue is whether the class structures of the 1970s remain a valid guide to those of the 1990s. What obtained during a golden age of capitalist expansion might crumble during a protracted recession, broken by intermittent, but jobless, recoveries. The class structure itself may be rearranged as some locations prove more viable than others. At an extreme, persistent involuntary unemployment may be or may become 'the central class divide in welfare state capitalism' (Van Parijs 1989:230). The current unhealthy state of the capitalist core's economies also reasserts some questions concerning the relative merits of Marxist- and Weberian-inspired class analysis previously answered using data from a more prosperous era. Wright (1989b:322) argues that 'Weberian class categories will have greater micro-level explanatory power under conditions of stable reproduction than under conditions of generalized economic crisis.'

So, in a somewhat less golden age, how do we make decisions concerning the location and strength of class boundaries for purposes of comparing the class structures of nations? The sensible response is to make those distinctions that are associated with patterns of social mobility in 'late' or 'managerial' capitalism. This offers both a final justification of our preference for the class structure as mapped by Goldthorpe, and the lead into the next chapter, which is concerned with patterns of social mobility.

Notes

1. Pawson (1989) offers the most compelling argument for the self-
   reinforcing qualities of explanation and measurement in sociology

generally. More specifically, class categories are embedded in one's theoretical perspective and, in Pawson's vision, evidence is used to exonerate 'not only the substantive theories but also the measurement and classificatory units that go to make up the theories' (1989:187).

2. The 'Golden Age' designation given is by Maddison (1982).

3. It would be preferable to have used Wright II for our purposes, but the relevant data are simply not currently available. Based on the matrix provided by Marshall *et al.* (1988:41), it is clear that the practical difference between using the 8-category Wright I schema obtained from Holtmann and Strasser (1990) and the 12-category Wright II is minor when our purpose is a comparison of class structures rather than predicting, say, class consciousness or income. Even there, it is unclear that the differences between the two class schemes would greatly affect the empirical results, whatever the consequences for the theoretical purity of an exploitation-based perspective on class (see Wright 1989a:34–41). This is because we are able to report an expanded version of Wright I, in which the class location of 'manager, advisory manager, and supervisor' is subdivided into its three components, as discussed in Chapter 3.

4. We regret that for France, Hungary, Ireland, and Japan we can report on the class structures only from the Goldthorpe perspective.

5. Szymanski does, however, acknowledge distinctions by qualification and work situation within the working class. Thus, routine white-collar workers are either clerical or not; blue-collar workers are either employed in production or in service.

6. For example, family capitalism flourished in Britain until World War II, long past its swan song in North America, and participation by family members in the top management of major companies remained prevalent in the period under consideration here (Chandler 1984/92:152).

7. Claims are also advanced for the significance of processes of de-skilling in services and manufacturing and of feminization of marginal class locations.

8. One of the historian J. H. Hexter's (1961:112–14) formidable 'reappraisals' restricts the true rise of the middle class to the period between the French Revolution and the English 1832 electoral reforms that allowed economic realities to find political expression. Yet middle-class pre-eminence was obviously preceded by a long and complex gestation. Certainly, Earle (1989) convincingly depicts a comfortable, entrenched, and differentiated English middle class in the late seventeenth century. The phrase 'middle class' was coined in 1785 'to refer to the propertied and largely entrepreneurial class located between landowners, on the one hand, and urban-industrial

workers and agricultural labourers on the other, in a society undergoing transition' (Abercrombine and Urry 1983:1).

9. For comparisons between the salaried and entrepreneurial middle classes, see Scase and Goffee (1982). The contemporary relevance of that divide is central to the work of Goldthorpe and Erik Olin Wright. The middle class has, however, always been internally differentiated. 'Middling sort of people' or the 'middle station' were phrases in use a century before Europe heard first of a middle class (Earle 1989). In the London of Defoe (1660–1730) three tiers within the middle class were commonly recognized: upper, middle class proper, and lower.

10. Whether the evidence supports claims of a structural reversal in the fortunes of the petty bourgeoisie remains contested territory (see Linder and Houghton 1990; Steinmetz and Wright 1990).

11. Other factors promoting a rising petty bourgeoisie include a decline in high-paying wage employment, and state policies (in taxation for example) that encourage small-scale entrepreneurship. Steinmetz and Wright (1989; 1990) downplay the importance of such considerations, while rejecting outright the possibility that rising self-employment is a countercyclical response to unemployment.

12. Gallie (1988:46–74) argues persuasively that the term underclass is not usefully extended to those who are simply disadvantaged within the labour market. See also Runciman (1990:388).

13. A Marxist formulation is broadly similar: the excluded sector is composed of all those who are presently unemployed and are neither part of a nuclear family with a full-time relation to the means of production nor whose life trajectory (student, job, temporarily unemployed, retired) is basically one of employment (Szymanski 1983:86).

14. And concluded that the same patterns emerge whether the unemployed are merged with other classes or treated separately (Goldthorpe and Payne 1986).

CHAPTER 5

SOCIAL MOBILITY

Introduction

Neither the position of families nor individuals within the class structure nor that structure itself, remain constant over time. Individuals and families change their class position and the class structure itself evolves, as some occupations decline and others become more numerous. Both these sorts of change have been intensively studied by sociologists and other social scientists. Examining the development of a class structure over time involves adopting a historical perspective, as in the work of Przeworski *et al.* (1980) or Wright and Martin (1987). The extent and the way in which families move through the class structure – between positions in it, in other words – is the subject matter of the study of social mobility. Social mobility has long been a central topic of sociological inquiry, and has been particularly actively pursued over the past 25 years. In this chapter our aim is to explain what the study of social mobility is, to give a brief explanation of the methods used in social mobility analysis, and to summarize the main results of recent research. Before we begin, however, we need first to set the scene by saying something about the temporal dimension of social class.

The temporal dimension of social class

There are a number of ways in which the temporal dimension of social class might be of relevance to us. We have already mentioned the phenomenon of people or families moving from one class to another: this is called social mobility, and examples of this are all around us. But there are other aspects to the temporal dimension of social class, of which we can identify three.

First, the relative sizes of social classes can change over time. We see examples of this during the twentieth century in Europe, where the class structures of many societies have changed markedly. Among men, agriculture and agricultural occupations have declined in significance, as has unskilled manual work, while white-collar jobs and skilled manual jobs have become more numerous. This kind of change is usually called 'structural' change – in other words, a change in the class structure.

Second, the nature of classes themselves can change over time. For example, is being a clerk in the 1990s really the same thing as being a clerk in, say, the 1920s? The answer is that it is probably quite different: in the 1920s possession of a clerical job probably led to a very much higher relative social standing and standard of living than it does nowadays. Similarly, the same argument might be made about professions which, over the years, have lost their standing in the community and which, in relative terms, have come to be less well paid – in Britain teaching is an obvious example.

A related issue has arisen in the so-called 'deskilling debate' in sociology. Here the argument was made by a number of sociologists – such as Braverman (1974) in America and Crompton (1980; Crompton and Jones 1984) in Britain – that the growth in the number of middle-class jobs and, particularly, skilled jobs, in the post-war period has been more apparent than real. This is because, so it is argued, the explosion in the number of so-called skilled jobs has been accompanied by their simultaneous deskilling. So, while what were formerly considered to be skilled jobs have indeed increased in number, their actual job content has shifted so that, in fact, these jobs nowadays require very little skill at all. Consequently, they are unlike genuine 'skilled' jobs in terms of the satisfaction they afford or the capacity they give workers to control the work process. Many of these new jobs are, in reality, low-skilled and repetitive.[1]

Third, the consequences and corollaries of class membership can also shift over time. In the terms we have been using, the social power deriving from class membership can change. So, for example, class differences in, say, mortality, or income might narrow or increase. Similarly, cultural and other differences between classes might also change, as well as behaviours considered to be linked to membership of a particular social class.

So, class is by no means necessarily a constant, and when sociologists carry out research that has a longitudinal or historical dimension, they have to pay a good deal of attention to issues such as the changing consequences of class membership. However, the temporal dimension has received most attention in the study of social mobility, and it is to this that we now turn.

Social mobility

When we examine social mobility – that is, how and why people or families change position in the class structure – we are usually interested in two things. First, in the nature of mobility: how much change in class position is there; how far do people move from their original class; is there more upward or downward mobility in society; how does mobility affect people's behaviour and attitudes (for example, when people are mobile out of class X and into class Y, to what extent do they continue to behave (for example to vote) in ways that are typical of class X – from which they have come – and to what extent do they take on the behaviour typical of the class to which they move – class Y?)? Second, we are interested in the consequences of mobility for the class structure. For instance, if we take one class virtually all of whose members have always been in that class and whose families were before them, and contrast it with another class which is chiefly made up of families which have been mobile into that class from outside it, how are the two likely to differ? In particular, will the members of the more 'closed' of the two classes be more likely to view themselves as constituting a class *for* themselves, in Marx's terms, than will the members of the more open class?

These two perspectives on mobility are, as we might have anticipated, not entirely distinct. Classes are, after all, made up of families and the individuals within them: they both comprise a class and are influenced by being members of it, in much the same way that individual actions are shaped by the existence of constraints but also help, to a greater or lesser extent, to change or maintain these constraints.

Inter-generational mobility

The most commonly studied form of class mobility is termed inter-generational mobility. This takes the form of a comparison of a person's current social class with the class that his or her family occupied at the time the person was growing up.

The vast majority of studies of inter-generational mobility have analyzed data for men: typically, then, the comparison is between the class position occupied by a man's family at the time he was growing up (say, at age 16) and the class position he currently occupies. When these studies are carried out on populations or large samples the relationship between the two is shown as a two-dimensional cross-tabulation (see Table 5.1). This table shows us the number of men who fall into each combination of current class and the class they were part of when they were growing up. Such tables are sometimes called origin by destination tables, since the name 'class origin' is usually given to the class they occupied when they were growing up, and 'class destination' is the name given to their current class. Hence the process of mobility is conceived of rather like a journey or a flow from an origin to a destination. The labelling of the two margins of the table in this way overcomes a problem of interpretation that had caused some problems in mobility analysis; this is that, despite the term 'inter-generational' mobility, the distribution of men across the origin classes did not represent the class structure as it was at any particular point in time or for any particular generation. Mobility data is gathered from a survey of men (or people) in the current population (sometimes only the current working population) and thus, if it is representative of that population, it cannot, in its distribution over

Table 5.1 Three-class mobility table: men in England and Wales 1972.

		Current (destination) class			
		1	**2**	**3**	**Total**
Origin class	**1**	731	322	189	1242
	2	857	1140	1109	3106
	3	787	1386	2915	5088
	Total	2375	2848	4213	9436

Classes are: 1 = Service; 2 = Intermediate; 3 = Working.
Source: Calculated from Goldthorpe *et al.* (1980/87), Table 2.2.

the origin classes, be representative of any other population (except by chance) – such as a particular generation or age group, or even of the population of fathers or families of men currently in the workforce (Duncan 1966). Therefore, mobility tables do not show us how one generation's class distribution evolves into the next generation's; rather, they show us how the classes men start out in (their origins) relate to the class they are in at the time of the survey (class destinations[2]).

Table 5.1 refers to a sample of 9436 men in England and Wales interviewed in 1972 for the Oxford Mobility Study (Goldthorpe 1980/87). It is immediately evident, of course, that what the table looks like will depend very much on how many classes we identify: here we have used a three-class categorization, and, as is conventionally the case, the same three classes are identified for origins as for destinations. These three classes are termed the service, intermediate and working class, respectively, and are defined as explained in Chapter 3.[3] The working class comprises men in largely manual occupations, whether these are considered skilled or not. The service class is made up largely of professionals, managers, administrators, supervisors of white-collar workers and owners of capital. In the middle, the intermediate class comprises other white-collar workers – such as clerical workers, salespersons, employees in services – small proprietors, such as farmers and smallholders, the self-employed (who do not employ others), and lower-grade technicians and supervisors of manual workers. [4]

This table tells us that there are 731 men who were born into class 1 and, at the time of the survey, were in class 1; there were 322 men also born into class 1 who had moved to class 2; and so forth. Since it is difficult to interpret what these numbers mean when they are presented this way, they are usually given as percentages. If we calculate the percentages along the rows, we get the percentage of all men of a given origin class in each destination class. This is termed an 'outflow' table. Such a table for the England and Wales sample looks like Table 5.2. This table tells us that, for example, of all men originating in the working class, 15 per cent moved into the service class; 27 per cent moved into the intermediate class; and the remaining 57 per cent stayed in the working class (they were 'immobile'). Another way of interpreting this is to say that the probability of a man, who was born into the working class moving into, say, the intermediate class, was 0.27.

Table 5.2 Percentage outflow mobility table: men in England and Wales 1972.

| | | Destination class | | | |
		1	2	3	Total
Origin class	1	59	26	15	100
	2	28	37	36	101
	3	15	27	57	99

Classes as Table 5.1. Percentages are by row – row totals may not add to 100 because of rounding.
  Source: As Table 5.1.

Table 5.3 Percentage inflow mobility table: men in England and Wales 1972.

| | | Destination class | | |
		1	2	3
Origin class	1	31	11	5
	2	36	40	26
	3	33	49	69
	Total	100	100	100

Percentages are by column – column totals may not add to 100 because of rounding.
  Source: as Table 5.1.

The other way of percentaging the table is to do it by columns: this gives us the percentage of men in a given destination class who come from the various origin classes. This is termed an 'inflow' table. An inflow table looks like Table 5.3. We interpret this table by, for example, noting that, of the current occupants of the intermediate class, 11 per cent came from service-class origins; 40 per cent came from intermediate-class origins; and 49 per cent came from working-class origins.

These two different ways of percentaging a table yield different insights into mobility. The inflow table tells us about the current composition of the classes, in terms of where members of the class came from. So, they tell us how heterogenous each class is in its composition. In these data an interesting contrast is provided by the service class and the working class. The service class is very heterogenous in its composition, being made up almost equally of men from all three origin classes, while the working class is much more homogenous: over two-thirds of men in this class were also born into this class. It is relevant to bear in mind that the service class expanded over this period – hence one would expect that it would be heterogenous in its composition not least because there are not enough men of service-class origins (1242 in Table 5.1) to fill the number of service-class destination positions (2375). Conversely, the working class destination is much smaller than the working-class origin, and the reverse argument applies. As the number of positions in this class contracted, we should expect that the remaining positions would have been filled by those with origins in that class, rather than by outsiders moving in.

We should expect, furthermore, that differences of this kind in the composition of classes would have consequences for the formation of 'class consciousness'. The members of a class which is relatively homogenous with respect to the class origins of its members are, all other things being equal, probably rather more likely to be aware of themselves as constituting a distinctive class than are the members of a class who are diverse in respect of their class origins.[5] 'In general, the greater the degree of "closure" of mobility chances – both intergenerationally and within the career of the individual – the more this facilitates the formation of identifiable classes' (Giddens 1973:107). However, shared class origins are only one factor which may contribute to an awareness of class (see Chapter 2 and Giddens 1973).

The outflow table, on the other hand, tells us the chances of ending up in a particular destination class, given that a man started in a certain origin class. We can then make a comparison of these chances as between different origins. For example, the chances of a man born into the working class getting into the service class are 0.15 or 15 per cent; while the chances of a man of service-class origins staying in that class are 59 per cent. So, men from the service class are much more likely to be found there than are men born into the working class. Hence, the outflow table provides us with a ready means of examining class differences in mobility chances, or, to put it in slightly different terms, the strength of the relationship between where you start out in the class structure (your class origin) and where you go to (your class destination).

However, when we make these comparisons of mobility chances as between different origin classes, we do not usually do so in terms of probabilities (or percentages flowing into a particular destination class from a given origin class); rather, we calculate chances in terms of odds. This idea will be familiar to any readers with an interest in gambling. Instead of looking at the *probability* that a man of intermediate class origins ends up in the service class, we look, instead, at the *odds* that such a man ends up in the service class *rather* than another class. So the probability of being in the service-class destination is .28, while the odds of being in that destination class rather than in, say, the intermediate class are 0.75. This figure is equal to the number (or percentage) who end up in the service class divided by the number (or percentage) who end up in the intermediate class.[6] So, when we make the comparison across different origin classes, we do this in respect of the odds of being in one destination class, rather than another. If we then want to compare the mobility chances of men from service-class origins with those of men from intermediate-class origins, say, we do this in terms of the odds of their arriving at one destination class rather than another.

For example, we can compare the odds of entering the service-class destination rather than the intermediate-class destination, as between men of service-class and intermediate-class origins. In these data, then, the odds for men of service-class origins are: 731 (= number of men in service-class destination from service-class origins) divided by 322 (= number of men in intermediate-class destination from service-class origins) = 2.27; while for men of intermediate-class origins they are 857 (= number of men in the service-class destination from intermediate-class origins) divided by 1140 (= number of men in intermediate-class destination from intermediate-class origin) = 0.75. We compare these two odds by simply taking their ratio: this yields a measure called the 'odds ratio' which, in this case, is equal to 3.03.

The odds ratio is the conventional measure of inequality in access to particular class destinations from different class origins. Odds ratios are usually set up so that they measure the odds of getting into a 'higher' or more desirable destination class, relative to getting into a lower, or less desirable, class. Odds ratios can be readily interpreted as a measure of how the odds of getting into a more desirable class relative to getting into a less desirable one

Table 5.4 All possible odds ratio in the three-class England and Wales mobility table.

Destination class	Origin class	Odds ratio
1 v 2	1 v 2	3.03
1 v 2	1 v 3	3.98
1 v 2	2 v 3	1.32
1 v 3	1 v 2	5.03
1 v 3	1 v 3	14.33
1 v 3	2 v 3	2.85
2 v 3	1 v 2	1.65
2 v 3	1 v 3	3.54
2 v 3	2 v 3	2.15

differ as between different origin classes. Equality of access to a more desirable, rather than a less desirable, destination class, as between different origin classes, would give rise to an odds ratio of one (since both origins would have the same odds). If the odds ratio is more than one, this reflects greater advantages to the origin class whose odds form the numerator of the ratio, while an odds ratio less than one indicates that the advantages accrue to the destination class whose odds form the denominator.

It might seem that there is likely to be a plethora of possible odds ratios that we could calculate for any table. In Table 5.4 we show all the possible odds ratios in the three-class table for England and Wales.[7] So, for example, the odds of being in the intermediate-class destination rather than the working-class destination are 2.15 times greater for men of intermediate class origins than for men of working-class origins. However, it turns out that not all of these odds ratios are independent of one another. In a mobility table using M classes (M = 3 in our example) there are $(M-1)^2$ independent odds ratios. So, in our three-class table, there are four independent odds ratios. If we know these, then we can calculate all the rest. So, for example if we take any pair of destination classes (say classes 1 and 3) we can calculate the odds ratio as between origin classes 2 and 3 (which is 2.85) from a knowledge of the odds ratios involving origin classes 1 v 2 (5.03) and 1 v 3 (14.03). In this case we divide the latter by the former to yield 2.85.[8]

Structural and exchange mobility

We have spent some time discussing odds ratios because they turn out to play a central role in mobility table analysis. We will now explain why.

Many mobility analysts have argued that the mobility we see in a mobility table can be explained as the result of two processes. These are sometimes called structural and exchange mobility. The idea behind structural mobility is quite simple. If we take a given society, the amount of inter-generational class mobility that we observe will depend, to a very great extent, upon the degree of change in the class or occupational structure of that society. So, a society which was developing rapidly should show a lot of mobility, not least because many occupations would be declining in importance and thus men whose father held one such occupation would have very great difficulty in pursuing the same occupation. They would, in a sense, be forced to be mobile out of that class or occupation by virtue of the fact that the occupational positions were not there for them to fill. Sometimes this kind of mobility is called 'forced mobility'. The difference between the origin class and destination class distributions in a mobility table is sometimes taken as a measure of the extent of this. So, in the three-class table (Table 5.1), we see many more origin than destination positions in the working class, and rather more destination than origin positions in the service class. So, the suggestion is that men must have had to move out of the working class because it is contracting, and, equally, men must have been 'drawn into' the service class as it expanded.

It was usually argued that this process operated independently of other processes of social mobility. In particular, it operated independently of processes of exchange mobility, which was concerned with how different class origins influenced mobility, and the inequalities in mobility chances that derive from different class origins. The reason that different origins confer different chances of mobility is because they provide people with different resources for mobility. So, people born into more advantaged classes generally acquire higher levels of formal qualifications, and, in addition, may have other resources (such as kinship links or friendship networks) which they can use to help them acquire a more desirable class position. In his analysis of the English and

Welsh mobility data Goldthorpe (1980/87:99) developed a mobility model in which he argued that patterns of social fluidity (in other words, patterns of inequality of access to particular class destinations as between men of different class origins) were shaped by three factors. These are, he argues, the *relative desirability* of different classes as destinations; the *barriers to entry* to these classes; and the *resources* attached to different class origins which allow these barriers to be overcome and the more desirable destinations to be entered (and the less desirable ones to be avoided).[9] So, people seek to gain entry to more highly desired destination classes: to do this they must overcome a variety of barriers to entry (such as the requirement to possess certain educational or other credentials; or the acquaintance of particular individuals), using the resources that they have acquired as a result of their origin-class position.

From this it follows that if resources were more or less equally distributed (so that the resources one had for mobility did not depend upon one's origin class) there should be a good deal of inter-generational class mobility in society. Hence, an egalitarian society (in the sense of one in which there was equality of condition as between people of different class origins) should be a society displaying high rates of mobility. In particular, of course, the chances of people born into a given class staying in that class would be no better than the chances of people born outside that class entering it. Therefore more equal societies should display more social mobility.

However, we have already seen that the amount of mobility in a society also depends upon the amount and speed of occupational or class change. Hence, a society which was very unequal could, it appeared, display a high rate of mobility provided that the pace of structural change were fast enough. The problem is to disentangle these two effects: how much mobility is due to structural change, and how much reflects the degree of equality – or, as it is sometimes called, openness – in society? The posing of this question then led to a number of attempts, by sociologists, to partition the total amount of mobility in a given observed mobility table into a component due to structural mobility (which was, in some fashion, linked to changes in the marginal distributions of the mobility table – that is, to the difference between the origin and destination distributions) and some component due to exchange mobility.[10] None of these attempts, in the 1970s and early 1980s, were particularly successful.

In the 1970s, however, a number of sociologists began to point out that odds ratios might be useful in this context, since they certainly measured inequalities in access to different class destinations arising from different class origins. Furthermore, odds ratios are independent of the marginal distributions of the mobility table. This means that, if two societies have the same level and pattern of class inequality in relative mobility chances, the fact that one of them has experienced rapid changes in the class structure (and, perhaps as a result, the origin and destination distributions are more unalike in one country's table than in another's) will not affect the fact that the pattern and magnitude of their odds ratios will be the same. Drawing on this, Goldthorpe and his co-authors (Goldthorpe 1980/87; Erikson, Goldthorpe and Portocarero 1979, 1982) abandoned the structure/exchange distinction and replaced it with an emphasis on absolute mobility (the actual mobility observed in the mobility table) and social fluidity (measured in terms of odds ratios), sometimes called 'relative mobility'.[11] There is no attempt, in this approach, to partition absolute mobility into some part due to structural change and some to exchange mobility.[12]

Nevertheless it provides a framework in which it is possible to identify societies which display very high rates of absolute mobility, together with low social fluidity or low 'societal openness' as reflected in large odds ratios. A very good example of this is provided by social mobility data for São Paolo, Brazil, collected by Hutchinson (1958) and later presented and used by Sobel, Hout and Duncan (1985:366). This shows massively high rates of absolute mobility, arising from very rapid and large changes in the class structure together with very large odds ratios reflecting a high level of inequality in access to more desired class destinations as between men of different class origins.

Absolute mobility

The study of absolute mobility places the focus on changes in the class structure over time (such as the contraction or expansion of classes). We have already noted the major trends in this respect during this century in most of the industrialized countries of the world: the decline in farming and farm-related jobs, and in unskilled work, with increases in skilled and white-collar jobs. The timing of this transition has, however, varied. We can gain some indications of this by comparing the origin and destination distributions for a number of tables from different countries.[13] Table 5.5 shows this comparison for four of the European countries taken from the CASMIN data set – Sweden, England and Wales, the Republic of Ireland, and Poland. Here we have moved to a five-class classification, in order to bring out some of the salient differences between these societies. These five classes (with the Erikson and Goldthorpe 11-class schema classes in parentheses) are:

1. White-collar workers (I, II, IIIa and IIIb).
2. Petty bourgeoisie (IVa and IVb).
3. Farmers and farm workers (IVc and VIIb).
4. Skilled workers (V+VI).
5. Non-skilled workers (VIIa).

(See Erikson and Goldthorpe 1992b: 38-9.)

We have chosen these four countries because they represent four different sorts of society – England and Wales having been industrialized for a long period, Sweden being a society which has experienced a long period of social democratic government and which has, accordingly, developed possibly the world's most comprehensive system of social welfare (broadly defined). The Republic of Ireland is a late-industrializing nation that retains a substantial dependence on agriculture, and Poland was, at the time these data were collected, a state socialist country.

Many of these differences are reflected in the comparison of the origin and destination distributions of their respective mobility tables. For example, it is noticeable that in England and Wales, origin classes 1 (white-collar workers) and 4 (skilled manual workers) are much larger (in percentage terms) than in the other three countries, reflecting Britain's earlier industrialization. In Sweden the destination distribution of class 1 is of comparable size

Table 5.5 Percentage origin- and destination-class distributions: Sweden, England and Wales, Republic of Ireland, Poland.

		Classes				
		1	2	3	4	5
Sweden	Origin	14	11	26	24	25
(N = 2103)	Destination	32	8	5	30	24
E & W	Origin	21	10	5	39	26
(N = 9434)	Destination	34	8	2	41	15
Republic of	Origin	11	10	39	14	27
Ireland	Destination	23	8	21	20	27
(N = 1992)						
Poland	Origin	10	3	53	18	16
(N = 32109)	Destination	20	2	25	31	22

Source: CASMIN data set.

to England and Wales, but in Ireland and Poland it remains much smaller. The relative lack of men in class 2 (petty bourgeoisie) in the Polish origin and destination distributions is hardly surprising in a state socialist country. In the other countries the distributions of this class are quite similar. It is in class 3 (farmers and farm workers) that we find major variation, particularly in the destination distributions where the contrast is between the two countries which retain substantial dependence on agriculture (Ireland and Poland) and whose industrialization has been very late and the other two. However, the decline in the importance of farming in Sweden has been both recent and very rapid indeed as we can see by comparing the origin and distributions for class 3 here. Conversely, agriculture declined in significance in England and Wales long before the period covered by these data: here class 3 makes up only a very small part of both the origin and destination distributions. Finally, class 5 (unskilled workers) shows a good deal of cross-national variation, particularly in a comparison of Poland with the other three countries. Here we see that it is relatively under-represented in the origins, but is the only country in which this class is larger (in relative terms) in the destination distribution. Again, it seems likely that the unusual position of Poland is associated with its post-war experience of state socialism.

Table 5.6 Percentage inflow tables from Sweden, England and Wales, Republic of Ireland, Poland.

		Destination classes				
		1	**2**	**3**	**4**	**5**
(a) Sweden						
	1	28	13	0	9	6
	2	12	23	5	10	8
Origin class	3	17	23	84	21	32
	4	24	19	5	30	21
	5	19	22	7	31	32
(b) England and Wales						
	1	37	18	11	12	15
	2	10	25	5	7	11
Origin class	3	3	4	67	3	9
	4	33	34	3	49	61
	5	17	20	13	29	5
(c) Republic of Ireland						
	1	28	9	1	9	5
	2	15	33	1	8	7
Origin class	3	21	30	92	14	33
	4	15	7	1	33	12
	5	21	21	5	37	43
(d) Poland						
	1	25	8	1	9	7
	2	5	18	1	3	3
Origin class	3	34	44	92	37	51
	4	21	16	2	30	16
	5	15	13	4	21	23

Source: As Table 5.5.

Table 5.6 shows the percentage composition of the destination classes in terms of origin class: in other words, the table shows what percentage of men in a given class come from each of the origin classes. We limit ourselves to highlighting two points. First, the class which has shown the greatest growth in these four countries – the white-collar class 1 – also shows substantial heterogeneity of composition. This is particularly striking in Ireland. Nevertheless, with the exception of Poland, the origin class which is most over-represented among the incumbents of this destination class is class 1 itself. This is part of a more general feature of these four tables, namely that for all except the relatively small classes, it is the corresponding origin class that supplies the largest share of members of a given destination class. The exception to this is Poland, where this is true only of the farming class.

The second trend is the remarkable degree of self-recruitment and class closure in class 3 (farmers and farm workers). This is particularly pronounced in Poland and Ireland, where this class remains very large. The reasons for this high degree of self-recruitment are easy to find: by and large farms are inherited, either legally or *de facto* and the same is true of jobs as farm workers. Except in England and Wales there is a good deal of mobility from class 3 into all the other classes, reflecting the 'forced' outward mobility of those born into a declining class.

On the basis of these figures, there is clearly no class in any of our four countries (class 3 excepted) in which self-recruitment could be said to lead to class closure sufficient to promote the formation of class consciousness. Class heterogeneity is particularly marked in Poland, largely because of the effects of the outflow from farming origins into the other destination classes.

Social fluidity

Sociologists interested in social mobility devote the majority of their attention to social fluidity. Recall that in studying social fluidity we are using odds ratios to measure the differences between people of different origin classes in their chances of access to more rather than less desirable destination classes. This is, therefore, a useful measure of the degree of societal openness, since if there were no differences in this respect between men of different class origins, all odds ratios would be equal to one. Such differences as exist are usually attributed to inequalities in the possession of mobility resources as between different class origins.[14]

When we come to try to judge whether or not a society displays much or little 'openness' of this kind, we can adopt one (or both) of two yardsticks. First, we could compare the observed set of odds ratios with the yardstick of total equality where all odds ratios would equal one. The latter is sometimes called a situation of perfect mobility, and it arises when there is no relationship between class origins and class destinations – that is to say, between the class a person starts out in and the one he or she is currently in. However, since all societies are some considerable distance from displaying perfect mobility, a possibly more useful perspective is provided by international comparisons which ask: How open is one society compared with another society?

One of the most famous hypotheses in sociology addresses exactly this question. The so-called Featherman-Jones-Hauser (FJH) hypothesis argues that a basic similarity will be found in social fluidity in all industrial societies 'with a market economy and a nuclear family system' (Featherman, Jones and Hauser 1975:340). This innocuous-seeming formulation has, if it is true, some very important ramifications. Many societies have expended a good deal of effort and resources on policies designed to increase societal openness by, for example, providing free education, medical care, and, more generally, the panoply of the welfare state. The FJH hypothesis suggests that whether a state pursues such policies or not has no consequences for the level of social fluidity that it will display.

The bulk of the many papers that have used comparative data to test the FJH hypothesis have arrived at much the same conclusions. These are that, first, the greatest differences between societies in mobility are in the area of absolute mobility. This is not surprising, given the different rates of structural change in societies, as we noted earlier. Second, there are very great similarities in the degree of openness in different societies. There are statistically significant differences in fluidity between them, but these tend to be relatively small for the most part. This finding has largely been born out by the results of the most painstaking and detailed comparative mobility project yet undertaken, the CASMIN project. In discussing the results of this research, Erikson and Goldthorpe find it necessary to modify the FJH hypothesis somewhat. Their conclusion is that:

> A basic similarity will be found in patterns of social fluidity . . . across all nations with market economies and nuclear family systems where no sustained attempts have been made to use the power of the modern state apparatus in order to modify the

processes or the outcomes of the processes through which class inequalities are intergenerationally reproduced. (Erikson and Goldthorpe 1987b:162)

What is notable about this modification is that, while retaining the emphasis on the high degree of commonality that apparently exists across industrialized nations in their pattern of social fluidity, it allows for the possible impact of state intervention. Erikson and Goldthorpe (1992b:178) argue that it is the attaining of greater equality of condition that best promotes high rates of social fluidity; that is, if inequalities in the conditions of life enjoyed by people are small, fluidity will be high. Thus, for example, policies of taxation and redistribution that seek to reduce the level of inequality in the distribution of income and in living standards, are likely, all other things being equal, to promote greater social fluidity.

Social fluidity in Europe

Differences in social fluidity will be most evident in comparisons involving the extremes. In Erikson and Goldthorpe's analysis of the CASMIN data the extremes of societal openness in Europe are represented by Sweden (most open) and Poland and the Republic of Ireland (least open), with England and Wales falling in the middle. In Table 5.7 we show the outflow tables for our four countries – Sweden, England and Wales, Republic of Ireland and Poland – with a view to comparing their social fluidity.

Recall that an outflow table tells us the percentage of men from each class origin who entered each destination class. So, in Table 5.7 we see that, in Sweden, of men born into class 1, 64 per cent had class 1 as their destination class. The striking feature of this table is that, for both white-collar (class 1) and skilled worker (class 4) destinations in all countries, the highest probability of being found in that class is enjoyed by men who were born into it. In all countries the strength of the link between origins and destinations in the white-collar class (as measured in this way) exceeds that observed in the farming class, and, in all countries except Ireland, so does the strength of this link among the skilled

Table 5.7 Percentage ouflow tables from Sweden, England and Wales, Republic of Ireland, Poland.

| | | Destination classes | | | | |
		1	2	3	4	5
(a) Sweden						
	1	64	7	0	18	11
	2	36	17	2	27	18
	3	21	7	17	24	30
	4	33	7	1	38	22
	5	24	7	2	36	31
(b) England and Wales						
	1	62	7	1	20	11
	2	37	21	1	25	17
	3	21	7	23	20	28
	4	29	7	0	41	23
	5	23	6	1	36	35
(c) Republic of Ireland						
	1	60	7	3	17	13
	2	35	28	3	15	20
	3	12	6	51	7	23
	4	25	4	1	47	24
	5	18	7	4	27	44
(d) Poland						
	1	53	2	1	29	15
	2	30	11	9	30	21
	3	13	2	42	21	21
	4	24	2	3	51	20
	5	20	2	7	40	32

Source: As Table 5.5.

working class. These figures suggest that in both these classes very effective mechanisms exist through which class position can be transmitted from father to son, despite considerable heterogeneity in the composition of these classes as destinations (particularly in the case of class 1, as revealed by the inflow table).

To undertake a proper comparison of social fluidity between these four countries would require that we model the pattern of odds ratios in each table using log-linear models, as Erikson and Goldthorpe (1987a and b, 1992b) do in their analyses. Here, however, we will compute some illustrative odds ratios.[15] So, for example, take the extreme odds ratios – that is the odds ratio of being found in destination class 1 (white-collar workers) rather than class 5 (unskilled manual) as between men of class 1 and class 5 origins. In Sweden this is 64/11 divided by 24/31 = 7.5. In England and Wales the ratio is larger – 8.6. In Ireland it is 11.3 and in Poland 5.7. On this basis, then, there is substantial inequality in competition for class 1 rather than class 5 destinations as between men of these different origins, but this inequality is least in Poland. However, the same is not true of the odds ratios of being found in class 1 rather than class 2 (petty bourgeoisie), given origins in class 1 rather than class 2. Here the figures are 4.3 for Sweden, 5.0 for England and Wales, 6.9 for Ireland and 9.7 for Poland. In other words, the disadvantages associated (in this case) with origins in the petty bourgeoisie are greatest in Poland, least in Sweden.

We could, of course, compute all the odds ratios in this table (all 100 of them) and compare them, but the general picture is as noted above. Odds ratios are, on average, smallest in Sweden, next smallest in England and Wales. Overall, Ireland has the next smallest odds ratios, followed by Poland. A simple index of this involves calculating these 100 odds ratios, taking their logarithm (so that an odds ratio of 1, indicating perfect equality, has a logged value of 0) and finding the average of the absolute values of these logged odds ratios.[16] The average for Sweden is 0.21; for England and Wales 0.24; for Ireland 0.30 and for Poland 0.33. Once again, using this particular yardstick, Sweden emerges as the society displaying the greatest social fluidity.

As we might expect, the explanation for the greater degree of social fluidity found in Sweden (not only by Erikson and Goldthorpe but by most other analysts of Swedish mobility in a comparative perspective: for example, Breen 1987; Erikson, Goldthorpe and Portocarero 1982; Erikson and Pontinen 1984) centres on the effects of a long period of social democratic government.[17] This has had the effect of reducing inequalities of condition (such as income inequality) and increasing equality of opportunity. In addition, the commitment to maintaining full employment seems also likely to have played a significant role in fostering high rates of social fluidity (Erikson and Goldthorpe 1992b:165).

By contrast, the low level of social fluidity in the Republic of Ireland is linked to a number of factors. Most important is

Ireland's position as a late industrializing, semi-peripheral state in which free post-primary education and very many other welfare state programmes were introduced only around the time that these mobility data were collected or afterwards. As a result, inequalities of condition between families were particularly marked (Breen *et al*. 1990) and thus, following Erikson and Goldthorpe's (1992b) argument cited earlier, a finding of low levels of social fluidity is perhaps not surprising.

What of Poland? Despite its post-war history Poland displays less social fluidity than either Sweden or England and Wales – but, once again, this accords with what we know of the impact of state socialism on social mobility. Broadly speaking, levels of social fluidity in state socialist societies are similar to those found in capitalist societies, albeit with some differences as to which classes are advantaged and which disadvantaged. Furthermore the persistence, in both Ireland and Poland, of a large agricultural sector in which inheritance is of overwhelming importance in acquiring a position as a farmer or farm worker, acts to reduce the overall level of social fluidity in these countries.

Finally, in our discussion of social fluidity we might ask: Where does America fit into this picture? A view of America as the 'land of opportunity' has existed for several centuries. In this view, America is seen as lacking the kind of rigid class structure felt to be characteristic of European societies and as presenting opportunities for personal advance that older countries could not. So, for example, the idea that class relations in America were distinctively different was found in Sombart's (1907/76) thesis of 'American exceptionalism'. While some studies can be seen as supporting this position (Miller 1960, and, particularly, Blau and Duncan 1967), recent research by Erikson and Goldthorpe (1985, 1992b:321) has led to the opposite conclusion: namely that 'no very convincing case for American exceptionalism . . . can be made out', and

> No matter how distinctive the United States . . . may be in (its) economic and social histories . . . or in the ideas, beliefs and values concerning mobility that are prevalent . . . it could not, on our evidence, be said that (it) differ(s) more widely from European nations in . . . mobility than do the European nations among themselves. (Erikson and Goldthorpe 1992b:337, parentheses added)

Conclusions

The study of social mobility is, we believe, a powerful research programme that tells us a great deal about the nature of modern societies and the position of classes within them.[18] However, it is hardly to be wondered at that, having been an area of active research for many years, it has generated many critiques. But what is less obvious perhaps is that the great majority of the criticisms levelled at mobility studies are not criticisms of mobility research *per se* but, rather, of the framework within which it is pursued. That is to say, most critiques of mobility research concern either the issue of the adequacy of the class classification used or the question of the appropriate unit of class composition. In this sense they are criticisms of mobility research *en passant*. Accordingly we deal with them elsewhere. We have already referred to some difficulties in the Goldthorpe class classification in Chapter 3. In Chapter 7 we address what is sometimes called the 'feminist' critique of class analysis (and, by extension, of mobility analysis), which centres on the argument that individuals, rather than families, are the appropriate unit of class composition.

Aside from these very important questions there are two specific criticisms of mobility research itself which we should mention. The first of these concerns the neglect of women in much social mobility analysis. It has been argued (by Hayes and Miller 1993 for example) that the concentration on men distorts the picture we have of mobility in modern societies. While this would be a very damaging criticism if it were true, there is much evidence to suggest that the inclusion of women in mobility studies does not change conclusions about social fluidity based on men-only studies (for example Marshall *et al*. 1988). While it is very obvious that there is a marked difference in the occupational and class distributions of men and women, patterns of social fluidity among women appear to be very similar to those found among men. In other words, differences in mobility chances between women of different class origins are much the same as those found between men of different class origins.

The second criticism is one which has been made by Poulantzas (1975) who argues that mobility research is fundamentally mistaken in placing its emphasis on the movement of individuals between class positions, when what should be focused on is the structure of, and the functions carried out by, these positions. While such as argument accords well with the views of 'structural Marxists' it is difficult to credit it with any force. In its concern with absolute rates, mobility research does indeed examine the structure of class positions in society. All researchers in the area accept, for example, that the single largest 'cause' of mobility flows during the last 100 years has been the contraction in the number of positions available in agriculture. On the other hand, in any society with a division of labour linked to unequal rewards the question of how people and families are distributed over these positions will be of central significance for an understanding of the way in which life chances are allocated. Furthermore, the study of how much openness of access exists to these various positions, as measured by social fluidity, tells us something very basic about the nature of the modern nation-state. To argue, as Poulantzas seems to, that a concern for such matters is misplaced is, at best, a statement of somewhat eccentric preferences.

Notes

1. These conclusions have been challenged and they are by no means generally accepted. See, for example, Goldthorpe 1980; 1982; 1985. We take this question up again in Chapter 7.
2. To label them class destinations may also be misleading, as Sorenson (1986) has argued. The men in a mobility sample typically range in age from 18 or 21 to retirement age or more, and their current class cannot be considered a destination (at least in the sense of final destination) for many of the younger men.
3. We could, of course, have used a finer class classification – say into seven classes, as Goldthorpe does for most of his analyses (see also Marshall 1990: Chapter 2).
4. The three-class categorization used here corresponds to that used by Goldthorpe *et al.* (1980/87) and not to that found in Erikson and Goldthorpe (1992b:38–9). In terms of the original Goldthorpe classes (as shown in Table 3.1) the three classes used here are made up as follows: Service class: I and II; Intermediate class: III, IV and V; Working class: VI and VII.
5. Recall that ease of mobility is one of the factors that Weber uses to distinguish the existence of social classes out of groups of economic classes.

6. So 28/37 from the outflow table (Table 5.2) is (allowing for rounding error) equal to 857/1140 from the original table (Table 5.1).

7. We could also invert all these odds ratios to yield a much larger total, but this would be of no interest.

8. We see why this follows if we write the odds ratio for any two origin classes in the form of a ratio, thus 1/2 and 1/3. It therefore follows that the ratio 2/3 is simply 1/3 divided by 1/2.

9. This example can be recast in the terms we used in our discussion in Chapter 1. Resources are used to overcome barriers (constraints) in order to try to secure the most desired destination (the most preferred alternative).

10. Some examples include Hazelrigg 1974; Hope 1981, 1982; and McClendon 1977, 1980. For a critique of this approach see Sobel 1983.

11. It was also recognized that odds ratios, which measure social fluidity, are directly captured in the parameters of log-linear models which, since the 1970s, have been used to model mobility tables (see Fienberg 1977; Goodman 1979). The parameters that are estimated in log-linear modelling fall into two kinds: main effect parameters, and interaction, or association, parameters. These latter depend upon the nature and extent of the statistical relationship between origins and destinations. Odds ratios are functions of these parameters, and not of the main effects. So, for example, if all odds ratios are one, the association parameters of the log-linear model will all be zero (in the log form of the model).

12. The structure/exchange distinction was then revived by Sobel, Hout and Duncan (1985). They present an elegant reformulation of the concepts, arguing that exchange mobility refers to equal reciprocal flows between pairs of classes (for example the flow from origin class A to destination class B and from origin B to destination A); and that structural mobility is captured in origin-specific parameters that make such flows unequal (so that the flow from A to B may, for example, exceed that from B to A). The difficulty with this model is that it implies that the observed mobility table should display the property of 'quasi-symmetry' (see Bishop *et al.* 1975 for a definition of this technical term). While a number of mobility tables do indeed display this property, many do not. In such cases, a third type of mobility – a residual category – has to be invoked in order to account for the observed flows.

13. It is important to reiterate that this only approximates changes in the class or occupational structures over time. To examine such change formally we should compare sample surveys of the labour force at two points in time.

14. Though, clearly, they might also be (and indeed, in reality probably are) due to differences in preferences for different class destinations among men of different class origins (in other words, in a relationship between origin class and subjective assessments of the desirability of different destinations).

15. As we noted earlier, odds ratios can be computed from either a table of frequency counts (Table 5.1 for example) or from tables of inflow or outflow percentages.

16. The technicalities of this measure need not concern us: interested readers should consult Breen 1994 for details.

17. Though Erikson and Goldthorpe (1992b:177–9) are at pains to argue that although state intervention may influence fluidity in particular instances (as in Sweden) this does not allow us to conclude that rule by a particular sort of political party (e.g. Social Democrats) will necessarily give rise to a distinctive pattern of fluidity in all countries where that kind of political party is in power. In other words, there does not exist, for example, a generic 'social democratic' pattern of social fluidity.

18. In this chapter we have concentrated on inter-generational mobility: however, in recent years a great deal of interest has arisen in the study of intra-generational mobility. While at its simplest this involves a tabular comparison of the class an individual occupied on entry to the labour force with the class he or she occupies at some later point in time (and is thus analogous to the origin – destination inter-generational mobility table), more sophisticated approaches are also used which seek to analyze the sequence and timing of transitions between jobs or classes that people experience during their life course (for example Allmendinger 1989).

CHAPTER 6

CLASS IN GEOGRAPHICAL PERSPECTIVE

Introduction

For us, one of the more challenging questions raised by class analysis is whether a social class inevitably begins and ends with a nation-state. We speak of a British class structure or a Swedish class structure, but we might equally argue that class structures have their origins in a global economy dominated by advanced capitalist enterprises. So might it be the case that the affinity between a member of the middle class in Britain and a middle-class Swede is greater than that which either has to their working-class or upper-class compatriots?[1]

This is a question that contemporary class theory and analysis typically ignore. The conventional, and convenient, practice is to associate a class structure with a nation-state – yet it is not self-evident that the nation-state is the most compelling level of analysis for the study of stratification. After all, Marx argued forcefully in *The Communist Manifesto* that the proletariat is an international class, with no economic or political interests at the national level:

> National differences and antagonisms between people are daily more and more vanishing, owing to the development of the bourgeoisie, to freedom of commerce, to the world-market, to uniformity in the mode of production and in the conditions of life corresponding thereto. (Marx and Engels 1977:235, first published 1848)

Most Marxist class theorists and analysts nevertheless share in the current preoccupation with class relations within specific nation-states (Vogler 1985:3), a sharp break from the assumptions made by Marx and Engels about the international nature of class struggle. There are exceptions: Wallerstein (1974, 1980, 1991) and Chase-Dunn (1989), adherents to a world-system perspective, stoutly maintain the tradition of a class struggle that is fundamentally international in scope.[2]

Why is the question of whether class and national boundaries coincide important? In our own model of stratification, advanced in Chapter 1, class is one of the bases shaping the distribution of social power and forms of consciousness. When we apply this model to the comparative analysis of class it directs attention to two issues. First, how do nations vary in the distribution of individuals and families across the class structure? Second, how do the consequences of class position vary cross-nationally? In Chapter 4 we addressed the first issue descriptively through examination of the class structures of a number of nations as depicted by the Wright and Goldthorpe schemata.

By explicitly focusing on the geography of class, this chapter seeks to understand the degree of cross-national differences in both the class structure and the consequences of class position. Are those differences primarily the result of factors specific to the individual nation-state or to more global forces and considerations? The world-system perspective, in which the stratification of nations rather than stratification within nations, is of primary concern, implies that international variation can be accounted for in terms of nations' positions in the world order. If this is so, then the ultimate base of class stratification is to be found not in the nation-state but in the economy of the world-system.

The stratification of nations and a world class structure

The world-system perspective is the primary body of thinking relevant to the relationship between a global economy and the status of national class structures, arguing that there is a division of labour among nations through which a core of countries mimics the role of the bourgeoisie and the periphery the role of the proletariat. A semi-periphery of nations approximates the uneasy role attributed to the middle class, simultaneously exploiter and exploited.[3] In its most influential expression by Wallerstein (1974) the world-system perspective regards the underdevelopment of peripheral countries as intrinsic to the world capitalist system, which is advancing on a road that leads to its eventual, and inevitable, demise. Contemporary national class structures are the products of each nation's position within the world economy and the associated form of labour control that it implies. Thus, for example, the traditional role of Latin American countries as suppliers of primary commodities renders the local bourgeoisie weak and ineffectual in realizing indigenous industrial development. The concentration of manufacturing enterprise in the core countries of Europe and North America, by contrast, fosters efforts at class compromise and the organization of workers through unions.[4]

The broad outline of a world class structure can be seen in the popular class-centred explanation for the emergence and persistence of this international matrix. Capitalists in the core countries appropriate surplus value from the periphery using cheap local labour to extract primary commodities ranging from gold to bananas and then exporting these to the core. Such appropriation can be accomplished without the need for sophisticated forms of labour control or a dynamic local bourgeoisie. The situation in the core of the system is very different. There, the development of manufacturing established 'creative class tensions' through a system of labour control that simultaneously nurtures an industrializing bourgeoisie and a politically strong working class (Ragin and Delacroix, 1979).[5]

The empirical status of such a sweeping perspective is necessarily equivocal. There are formidable difficulties in simply dividing countries into three mutually exclusive categories representing core, semi-periphery, and periphery. Then, too, there is the awkward position of countries like Ireland and Portugal located at the 'periphery of the centre', and of the rapidly industrializing East Asian countries such as Singapore and Indonesia that form a kind of 'centre of the periphery'. The placement of the 'Second World' comprised of the formerly state socialist countries is also inelegant.

It nonetheless makes sense to recognize the artificial quality inherent in any study of national stratification systems that does not acknowledge interdependencies among nations within the capitalist system. A strong case is put forward by Chase-Dunn:

> Classes are conventionally understood in terms of their operation within national societies, and class struggle is therefore seen as taking place primarily within countries. Objective economic classes cut across national boundaries to form a structure that can only be understood in terms of the world-system. (Chase-Dunn 1989:242)

In his systematic restatement of the world-system perspective, Chase-Dunn pairs the territorial core/periphery hierarchy with the world class structure (1989:38–43). Core, semi-periphery, and periphery are defined by the form of economic production that is dominant. A broad-stroke division of that kind can be traced back to the sixteenth century. Economic production in the core is capital intensive, while that in the periphery is labour intensive. The semi-periphery consists of regions in which economic production takes place through a balanced mix of core and peripheral production or is 'predominately intermediate' in nature (1989: 346–8).

Each form of production is linked to a type of labour-capital relationship. Core production is typically undertaken by highly skilled, well-paid labour. Peripheral production, which produces commodities using technology that is low in capital intensity, typically requires little skill and is undertaken by workers who receive low wages and are exposed to political coercion. The bottom-line to all of this is that 'the world class system may be best understood as a continuum from protected labour through wage labour to coerced labour which roughly corresponds to the core/ periphery hierarchy' (Chase-Dunn 1989:39–40). Protected labour is found almost exclusively in core countries and benefits from a framework of trade unions, corporatist institutions, labour regulations, and immigration controls that offer both protection from competition in the world labour market and a reasonable footing with which to engage capitalists. Wage labour is found to varying degrees throughout the world-system. The labour market determines wages and working conditions. Coerced labour is subject to the logic of profit-making by a variety of institutional means, and wages and working conditions are thus held below what the operation of free labour markets would generate.

It follows from this that the stratification system of any particular nation is conditioned to some degree by that nation's place in the world-system. A country's location in the world-system affects, for example, the coherence and competence of its bourgeoisie, the relative advantage enjoyed by capital over labour, and the role of the state and state institutions in mediating class relations.[6]

What practical significance does this have for the study of social stratification? If capital is global, for example, it follows that specific class positions do not unambiguously fit into national stratification systems. But the crux is that while capital is international, political structures, including trade unions, are national. It follows from this that living standards are more influenced by an international struggle among nations to raise each country's total national income than by a class struggle with capital itself. Neo-corporatism is one variant of what Vogler terms 'class-divided nation-states' in which 'domestic class relations are mediated primarily by a state's position in the world market and only secondarily by the balance of organized class forces within the nation' (Vogler 1985:xiv). Both workers and capital within a country optimize their position by rallying around their nation-state's fortunes. However, the march of integration within the world economy has the potential to form trans-national classes because workers of various countries are now linked directly through the production process, while national political institutions cannot protect them from market forces at the international level (Vogler 1985:xiii). Overall, though, prospects for the internationalization of class struggle remain slight.[7]

The relevance of the world-system perspective for the study of stratification is less dramatic, but important. At the top of the class structure a plausible case can be made that a world, rather than a national, capitalist class will emerge, unfettered by national allegiances and unhindered by national borders. Certainly the feasibility of organized class action on the international scene is greatest here. Still, the identity between the bourgeoisie and the nation-state is strong. To establish themselves and to compete with one another, states competed for capital. Max Weber observes:

> Out of this alliance of the state with capital, dictated by necessity, arose the national citizen class, the bourgeoisie in the modern sense

of the word. Hence it is the closed national state which afforded to capitalism its chance for development – and as long as the national state does not give place to a world empire capitalism will also endure (Weber 1961:249; quoted in Collins 1992:103).

Moreover, the contemporary world-system is 'multicentric', with a core consisting of competing nation-states. In Chase-Dunn's (1989:41) view, 'No state represents the "general" interests of the capitalist class as a whole. Rather, subgroups of the world capitalist class control particular states.' And within nation-states of all hues the capitalist class is often fractured (Bottomore and Brym 1989).

A world working class is even less easily comprehended. An international perspective on the working class, however, offers another explanation for the quiescence of the working class in the capitalist core. Capitalists and workers in the core of the world-system share an objective interest in perpetuating the exploitation of the peripheral countries. The profits of exploitation help to fund the welfare and higher wages enjoyed by workers in the capitalist core. Similarly, the geographic division of labour concentrates 'clean' and 'skilled' employment in the core countries. To Chase-Dunn (1989:43), conventional Marxist analysis exaggerates the contribution made to class harmony by the 'false consciousness' induced by nationalism and other ideologies. Shared interest in preserving world-system inequalities explains, in part, the disappointing response to the socialist alternative and the absence of class struggle under advanced or monopoly capitalism.

Of course, a partnership in exploitation between capital and labour in the core countries weakens the potential for a world proletariat, at least as a 'class for itself'. That may be a temporary *rapprochement*, however. If the grip of the capitalist core on the world-system were to falter, then the wage differential between workers in the core and periphery would presumably weaken. This, in turn, offers the potential for class disharmony in the core and greater worker solidarity across national boundaries (Chase-Dunn 1989:43). However, the multicentric nature of the world-system's core argues against such an outcome. Anti-capitalist energies are diffuse rather than concentrated. Where the prerogatives of capital are significantly challenged by workers, capital flight will simply lead to the particular nation-state's decline *vis-à-vis* the rest of the core (Chase-Dunn 1989:42).

National class structures in the world-system

Knowing where a country fits within the world-system would seem to speak directly and practically to the relative size of various classes. Specifically, the bourgeoisie will be smaller and the unskilled manual working class larger in the periphery and semi-periphery than in the core. There are also consequences for the interrelationship between the polity and economy of those countries, with a tendency to exclude the middle class from attaining the political power commensurate with its enhanced economic position (Mouzelis 1986).

The world-system perspective necessarily assumes, or assigns pre-eminence to, what is common to countries in the core, in the semi-periphery, and in the periphery. Other perspectives highlight the wide divergence among countries within each segment of the world-system, divergences that expand rather than diminish with the maturating of the capitalist system. The capitalist core, for example, is far from being a monolith:

> The advanced capitalist societies are regulated by institutions that hardly existed in the era of industrialization: the welfare state, collective bargaining systems, mass education, and the modern corporation have emerged as important, if not decisive, institutional filters. Nations vary dramatically with regard to these regulatory institutions, and it is therefore naive to assume convergent trends in employment and stratification. (Esping-Andersen 1993:8)

It follows that the individual nation-state remains the major delimiter of 'geographic specificity' within the capitalist system. And perhaps the middle class is most clearly nationally situated given the contemporary prevalence of state employment.[8]

Two tendencies within capitalism during the twentieth century had great significance for stratification systems. One was the internationalization of trade and the rise of the transnational corporation, as well as the drive towards European integration. But any consequent impetus towards a stratification system less securely based in the nation-state was in our view counterbalanced by a second trend: the link between state institutions and national stratification systems strengthened with the evolution of the welfare state and corporatist arrangements. As Esping-Andersen (1993) observes, because of the variety of ways in which welfare can be structured, the product of this enhanced link between state and class is diversity rather than homogeneity at the core of the world-system.

The end of the golden age puts the national balances achieved in various countries under welfare capitalism into doubt. Trade union movements are certainly weaker and welfare state institutions less secure in the 1990s. Whether this interregnum will usher in a new phase to the world-system, and thus in capitalism, or a minor reshuffling of the rank ordering of nations within the capitalist core is difficult to say at present. Nation-states are competing for mobile capital in ways that have demonstrable importance for the occupational structure of countries across the range from advanced core capitalist to the periphery. Decisions on the location of manufacturing production by large corporations do internationalize the relationship between capital and labour. This parallels the growth in the capitalist core of part-time, temporary workers who are both paid less and are less 'protected' than traditional core workers (Burawoy 1985:264–5).

A world-system perspective also highlights the stratification effects that flow from the migration of both labour and capital. In Western Europe and in the Americas the relationship between core capital and peripheral labour is basic to understanding immigration specifically, and more generally the ethnic dimension to stratification and how it interacts with class-based stratification.

However, world-system theory is rather poorly integrated with theoretical and empirical work on class stratification. This applies with particular force to the relationship between class theory and theory associated with the sociology of development:

> A situation has therefore emerged in which writers analyzing social stratification in the advanced countries take the nation-state as their unit of analysis, while those analyzing international factors (i.e. development theorists) document their effect on class relations in the less developed countries but not in the advanced nations. (Vogler 1985:6; see also Agnew 1987:232)

One response to the lack of a persuasive geography of class stratification is to look at the big picture, as Scase (1992) does. For Scase, in effect, what is similar among capitalist (or, alternatively, state socialist) countries is by definition what is important, and what differs can be treated as matters of minor, and inconsequential, detail. A second approach is to adopt a more formal model of comparative research. Here, the most fruitful perspective appears to be one that makes assumptions that limit the supranational factors that the study of stratification must bear: 'class analysis must take a given structural context as its starting point and concentrate on the elucidation of the processes occurring within that context, mobility included' (Goldthorpe 1990:412; see also Parkin 1979:114).

We choose to pursue the question of the implications of world-system theory for stratification by examining the recent situation in Eastern Europe. This offers us two points of entry into two 'naturally occurring' experiments in stratification, the first established by the creation of state socialism in the Eastern Bloc and the second by the breakdown of that mode of production at the close of the 1980s (Erikson and Goldthorpe 1992b:395).

Stratification under state socialism

Eastern Europe is fertile ground in which to investigate the geography of stratification. That is because we find there in the post-World War II era the confluence of three supra-national bases of stratification. One base is the area's status as a part of the world-system's semi-periphery. The second base is regional, a distinctive cultural, economic, and political arena with a common history. The third base is the experience of state socialism, an alternative mode of production to capitalism.

Chase-Dunn (1989:212) argues that there are two 'analytic kinds' of semi-peripheries. The variety represented by Eastern Europe is one where there is a balanced mix of core and peripheral activities. It is here that class becomes a potential basis for class action and revolution: 'More stratified semiperipheries are likely to produce social revolutions which challenge the logic of capitalism' (Chase-Dunn 1989:213). This assertion is perhaps most compelling when applied to the Soviet Union. It has some resonance, however, for the Eastern European countries that were in the Soviet sphere of influence, as well as military occupation, after World War II.

Eastern Europe as a region has historical roots in the Austro-Hungarian Empire and as the buffer between East and West, as well as the shared experience of post-war domination by the Soviet

Union. That region's countries are diverse in terms of their level of industrialization, the role of the state in effecting industrial expansion, and the extent to which agricultural land was retained as private property. So the region offers extensive variations on a somewhat muted common theme, with as much, if perhaps more obscure, diversity as that found among Western European nations.

State socialism presents a very different 'institutional mediation of power', to use Giddens's terminology, than that of capitalism. Specifically, in capitalism the market is given substantial sway because of the separation between the economy and polity. By contrast, the subordination of the economy to 'the directive control of the political administration, via the abolition of private property' should break the link between market capacity and class structuration that prevails in capitalist Western Europe (Giddens 1973:252).

To a large extent the state socialist countries of Eastern Europe opted out of the world economy. Yet, as we observed in Chapter 4, researchers undertaking comparative studies of stratification are comfortable applying identical class categories to capitalist and state socialist societies alike. Capitalism implies a class society. If that is a meaningful observation, then presumably state socialist societies imply something different. Even before the collapse of state socialism, most observers regarded Eastern Europe and the Soviet Union as class societies. In this view, the ownership of the means of production found in capitalist societies is merely a special case of the general concept of 'control over the labour of others' in the process of class formation (Böröcz 1989). State socialism is thus also a class society. However, the processes of class formation and the consequences for life chances of class membership were viewed as distinctive to state socialism.

The relationship between market capacity and life chances is altered under state socialism. Overall, the level of income inequality is lower in the Soviet Union and Eastern Europe (as best the available evidence can reveal) than in the capitalist core countries (Przeworski 1991:119, footnote 42). The two main differences between East and West are distributional:

> one is the higher relative income of manual workers, measured in terms of wages alone; the other is that lower white-collar workers do not enjoy the same pronounced advantages in terms of other

forms of economic return – job security, fringe benefits, etc. – which have traditionally distinguished manual and non-manual labour in the capitalist societies. (Giddens 1973:230)

In state socialist societies, therefore, unskilled white-collar workers form the bottom of the earnings hierarchy. The consequences of that positioning for social mobility, however, are largely negated by the advantage that white-collar workers have in access to education and, more generally, possession of cultural capital (Teckenberg 1990).

State socialist societies offered through 'income in kind' better doctor/patient and teacher/student ratios than in the West, but:

> these state redistributed benefits also functioned as means to differentiate, rather than reduce, the disparities associated with various positions in the social structure. (In the face of shortages) one simple and efficient way of rewarding rulers and their immediate subordinates was to allocate scarce infrastructural resources like access to good quality subsidized housing, personal services and the like to members of those classes . . . incomes in kind came to be of great importance as markers of class position. (Böröcz 1989: 281–2, parentheses added)[9]

On balance, overall inequalities were perpetuated across generations within the same families despite diminished inequalities in earned incomes. State policies shaped relative mobility chances in a manner that approximates what is observed in the capitalist core. Certainly there is neither a state socialist pattern to social mobility nor a tendency towards greater openness in the class structure in Eastern Europe (Erikson and Goldthorpe, 1992b).[10] Eastern European countries differ among themselves in their mobility regimes: they present, generally minor, variations on a general theme that can be traced to specific policies and programmes in each country. In terms of openness:

> the rate of upward mobility into service-class positions does rise quite sharply among the cohorts of men who reached occupational maturity during the immediate post-war period of 'socialist reconstruction' – but . . . with later cohorts, the rate then falls away. (Erikson and Goldthorpe 1992b:373)

What role did class stratification play in the demise of state socialism? It is ironic, but commonplace, to assert that the class structure of state socialist societies was polarized into two classes:

a dominant bureaucratic class of planners (Burawoy and Lukács, 1992:146–7) – that appropriated and redistributed the surplus created by the efforts of a class of direct producers. What differs most sharply from the Western democracies is the underlying, and supporting, ideology for the appropriation of surplus value. In capitalism, the appropriation of surplus value is legitimated by the market. Under state socialism, the legitimating ideology is that the centralized appropriation is being undertaken in the common interest.

Burawoy and Lukács use this to develop a conundrum of sorts by arguing that the capitalist regime of production generates consent, while that of state socialism promotes dissent. The operative ideology under state socialism clearly and forcefully portrays that central appropriation as being undertaken in the common interest. Such appropriation is highly visible, in contrast to the opaque class relations of late capitalism, as are the sharply differentiated consequences for life chances.[11] So it was under state socialism that polarization and class structure promoted the overthrow of the pre-existing system.

Another class-specific contributing factor was the growth over recent decades of the 'intermediate stratum' in all of the state socialist countries: 'the well-educated professional, technical and administrative personnel' (Bottomore 1991:81). That stratum:

> although its interests were to some extent bound up with those of the ruling group, had nevertheless a strong interest in economic and political reforms which would create opportunities for personal initiative and innovation, greater economic efficiency and a more liberal regime in which critical debate about social policies and problems could take place. (Bottomore 1991:81)

In this way, too, class stratification contributed to the demise of state socialism.

The consequences of the demise of state socialism in Eastern Europe are still being worked through; it is a region in flux. As 'experiments in destratification' (Lenski 1978) the recent Eastern European experiences leave behind a confused legacy that the passing of time may not help to untangle.

What does the future hold for class stratification in Eastern Europe? A possible window into the future is provided by Haller *et al.*'s (1990) use of the comparative study of social mobility in two regions that subsequently became nations – the Czech lands and

Slovakia – along with Austria and Hungary in order to test the relative importance of industrialization and political system effects. Historical differences between the two regions of Czechoslovakia in terms of the size of the agricultural sector and (from 1968) regional political autonomy (1990:163–4) justify their separate consideration. Also, 'until the end of the first World War Slovakia belonged to the Hungarian part of the Austro-Hungarian Empire, and has an educational system more similar to that of Hungary than to the Czech lands' (1990:167). The analysis of mobility patterns concludes that the two regions that once comprised Czechoslovakia were indeed unique due to 'specific historical and structural peculiarities' (1990:191). It seems unlikely, therefore, that the transition to capitalism will generate a distinctive Eastern European brand of class stratification.[12]

The former Soviet Union presents the most tangled knot with which to contend. Burawoy, whose perspective on class stratification was described in Chapter 2, argues that the former Soviet Union is experiencing a transition to merchant capitalism, rather than to industrial capitalism. In Burawoy's terminology, this entails a combination of anarchy in both the relations in production and the relations of production. Managers under industrial capitalism are uncertain about markets (and, therefore, about the relations of production). Under state socialism, managers were secure in the market for what they produced, but faced uncertainty about the quantity and quality of available materials, technology, and labour with which to produce (the relations in production). Burawoy asks: 'What happens when the party state first withdraws from the economy and then disintegrates leaving enterprises with greater autonomy?' (Burawoy and Krotov 1992:21).

The answer is a form of 'dual anarchy' in which neither markets nor production can be planned by managers or entrepreneurs:

> That new order is based on domination by monopolies whose powers reside in control of access to supplies . . . this economic system is driven by the pursuit of profit that comes primarily from trade rather than from transforming production. Work is in effect 'put out' to worker collectives in enterprises. (Burawoy and Krotov 1992:35)[13]

This has two main consequences. First, monopolies, barter, and worker control effectively inhibit the development of competition and markets. Merchant capitalism lacks an internal dynamic that will generate a 'take off' to industrial capitalism. Second, the economic effect is centrifugal, devolving control over commodities and trade to regions, thus encouraging the shift towards regionalism and localism in the former Soviet Union.

Other countries of Eastern Europe are more diversely situated in terms of their prospects for making the transition to democratic institutions and prosperity, relatively speaking. Their individual experiences will doubtlessly be imprinted on their class structures.[14] However, all of Eastern Europe shares with the countries of the 'South', notably Latin America, a difficult challenge:

> The bare facts are that the Eastern European countries are embracing capitalism and that they are poor. These are conditions Eastern Europeans share with masses of people all over the world who also dream of prosperity and democracy. Hence, all one can expect is that they too will confront the all too normal problems of the economics, the politics, and the culture of poor capitalism. The East has become the South. (Przeworski 1991:191)

So in the geography of the world-system, Eastern Europe is perhaps as closely linked to Latin America as it is to France, Germany, and Great Britain.

The nation-state and stratification

It appears, then, that the world-system plays a secondary role in shaping national patterns of stratification. The impact of the world-system on stratification is restricted precisely because of the extent to which states currently filter world-system effects. That conclusion reinforces the emphasis that should be given to the role of individual states and their policies in the study of class stratification.

What state policies serve as the filter? They are the ones captured by the label 'welfare state', if it is correctly defined in a broad sense. Welfare state polices do more than ameliorate the plight of indigents, the incapacitated, and the elderly. Rather, welfare states confer social citizenship, a guarantee of socially acceptable living standards independent of those which individuals experience as a consequence of market forces (Castles 1988; Myles 1988; Esping-Andersen 1990). The welfare state, and the policies and programmes that constitute it, can take diverse forms:

It can take the form of tariff protection, designed to cushion the impact of competitive market forces on wage levels or it can assume the character of industrial restructuring measures aimed at ensuring that individuals do not find themselves dependent on low-wage employment. It can focus on creating the conditions of full employment or it can provide compensation for those who cannot obtain jobs It can seek to control wage levels or it can use state action to redistribute income through the tax-transfer system. (Castles 1988:ix)

These are essentially alternative ways of achieving a single broad objective. That objective is to de-commodify individuals by making their living standards independent of pure market forces (Esping-Andersen 1990:3). So the capitalist labour market will not provide employment for all individuals, but state policies intervene to create jobs or to give financial compensation to those unable to find work. Typically, in fact, all advanced societies adopt policies that will both generate employment opportunities and support the unemployed. It is through the provisions of the welfare state, broadly defined, that individual nation-states mediate the impact of the world capitalist order on their citizens.

States vary, however, in their ability to implement such de-commodification. It is unfortunate (although perhaps not coincidental) that the nations for which we have extensive information on stratification, class structure, and class mobility are all ones that have some form of extensive de-commodification in their policy regimes. This is one reason why we believe that the world-system perspective might emerge as being far more important if we could extend our empirical studies to the developing world.

Even within the restricted range of countries subjected to class analysis, states are under varying degrees and forms of pressure to enhance competitiveness through commodification. Welfare states are therefore necessarily compromises between these two objectives. Nations display a diversity of policy packages through which to achieve such compromise. This leads, in turn, to different stratification consequences.

Esping-Andersen (1990) proposes three 'worlds' of welfare capitalism, each representing a distinct institutional structure of welfare state policies. The distinctions are based on (1) the principles underlying their interaction with market forces and (2) their impact on class inequalities and cleavages.

Conservative welfare regimes reject the cash nexus associated with the market and attempt to preserve or reconstruct community, hierarchy, and status differentials. In its 'corporatist' variant, social policies are divided according to occupational- and status-based programmes that differ in their benefit level. In the *'etatist'* variant, the primary beneficiaries of such favouritism are civil servants, maintaining a status barrier between state employees and private sector workers. Austria, France, Germany, and Italy exemplify key features of such a regime. *Liberal* welfare regimes are guided by a belief in the benefits that follow from unrestricted markets. Minimal interference with the market and the replication of market inequalities leads to means-tested and stigmatized relief limited to 'market failures' and a heavy reliance on private market-based welfare for more advantaged groups. Prime examples of this regime include Australia, Canada, and the United States. *Socialist* welfare regimes are guided by the aspiration to extend democratic rights and by the political imperative to construct solidarity. Socialist policies tend therefore to be universalistic in their coverage, with entitlement set at average or middle-class levels. Such a regime is most closely approximated by the Scandinavian countries.

In practice, the welfare states of advanced nations[15] contain elements drawn from more than one of these ideal types. The stratification consequences are thus complex. For example, a commitment to full employment might well augment the ranks of Goldthorpe's routine non-manual class in a country with a socialist welfare state regime and in one with a liberal slant. The effect on the shape of the class structure would thus not differ. But, if such employment were created largely in the public sector in the socialist welfare state country and in the low-wage private service sector in the liberal welfare state country then the consequences for the occupants of the routine non-manual class might differ considerably. In particular, the differential in life chances between them and the occupants of, say, the service class, would probably be much greater in the liberal than in the socialist example. This extends to the chances of upward social mobility, and thus to the degree of class structuration.

Linking state policy to class consequences within real, rather than hypothetical, regimes, however, is problematic. The strongest evidence for such a link concerns class abatement, in which state policies set an upper limit on the magnitude that class-based inequalities in key life chances can assume. To a degree that varies across countries, state policies in health care, education, social security, and taxation reduce class inequalities in life expectancy, educational participation rates, standards of living, and income.

Associating specific welfare state measures with the shape of the class structure or with social mobility is considerably more difficult. State policies represent but one of a range of socio-historical processes that determine the distribution of the population among classes at any point in time. This has led Goldthorpe (1990:417), among others, to argue that in attempts to understand the evolution of class structures over time, 'we must look far more to *historical* accounts of their particular forms, patterns of change and diversity than to theoretical ones.' Similar difficulties confound attempts to tie specific policy initiatives to social fluidity. While it is plausible to assume that particular policies may enhance mobility chances, conclusive evidence is absent.

It is reasonable to conclude that, on balance, a world-system perspective does not invalidate the comparative study of discrete national stratification systems. This applies with considerable force even within the restricted field of Eastern Europe. The stratification systems of the former state socialist regimes and the fledgling class structures that are taking their places all follow paths that make sense only within the confines of national histories. Stratification theory and research, however, will be artificial and sterile without reference to what is termed the 'interactive vision' (Evans and Stephens 1988) in which the effect of global economic forces is contingent upon national social structures. This is evident in the importance of specific economic and political factors that affect the rigidity of class boundaries and relations among classes and the interplay between those specifics and the general. This requires that we acknowledge:

> first, that there are variations in the labour process and particularly its political regime both within a given capitalist society and between capitalist societies; and, second, that these variations may be understood in terms of the historical constellation of struggles and competition as shaped by insertion into world capitalism. (Burawoy 1985:68)

It is instructive that neither these variations in the capitalist West, nor those found in Eastern Europe during and after the period of state socialism, appear to greatly affect social mobility. Insofar as social mobility is the main vehicle for what Giddens (1973) terms 'mediate structuration', the international context is almost by definition of secondary importance in understanding contemporary stratification. But that judgement may change as stratification research expands its horizons to Asia, Latin America, and Africa, and confronts processes of fragmentation (such as the demise of the Soviet Union) and integration (as manifest in the European Union) that are now underway.

Straws in the wind: Transcending the nation-state?

Perhaps the strongest rationale for studying the class structures of nation-states is the role played by state policies in education and industrial relations in shaping both class structure and the consequences of class membership. Yet we live in a period of geographical integration and fragmentation that may eventually unsettle the comfort that working with nation-states affords students of class stratification.

The recent European experience, after all, is dominated by change processes in which nation-states fragment or pursue avenues of integration into supranational entities. This complicates the association of class structures with nation-states. In 1989, for example, the Soviet Union clearly had a class structure. Today, do Russia, the Ukraine, and Belarus all possess separate class structures? Moving in the opposite direction, did German reunification unite two class structures for purposes of class analysis? Presumably so, but if that merger could be effected so abruptly it calls into question the geographical assumptions through which students of stratification operate. Certainly, such dramatic changes within so limited a time-span challenge the immutable quality of the link between nation-states and class structures. Similarly, the process by which the meaning of membership in the European Union is now being redefined, and the Union expanded to embrace Eastern and Northern Europe, weakens the link between state policies and stratification consequences. How far this will proceed is uncertain, but the stakes for those who study class stratification are substantial precisely because so much is based on the convenient assumption that class structure and nation coincide.

What are some of the possible implications? One is that processes of geo-political change may currently be changing the location of the primary institutions that shape stratification. Control over aspects of some of the key policy areas – education, industrial relations, taxation – is gravitating upwards to a decision-making apparatus that transcends the nation-state. Simultaneously, policy and economic realities are shifting the focal points of commerce and corporate management away from national centres and towards regional 'poles of prosperity' that are truly transnational, such as the Rhône-Alpes region centred around Lyons, France. The result, to some journalist commentators, is a concentration of economic might that harkens back to the city-states of the Hanseatic League, which thrived during the fifteenth and sixteenth centuries (Drozdiak, 1994).

A second implication concerns the enhanced possibilities for immigration among advanced capitalist societies. With the advent of the European Union, for example, it is less plausible to assume that those born into a national class structure will come to occupy a position within that structure and then remain within that structure throughout their working life. Careers may increasingly span class structures that we currently think of as being self-contained, with the class of origin, first destination, and final destination each being located within a different national class structure.

Third, the interactions between class stratification and that based on ethnicity, race, or gender may be clearest when viewed in reference to a specific region or place. This means that some of the criticisms made of class analysis refer to phenomena that are perhaps not best analyzed on the national level, but instead require analysis based on other geographic units. This fuels the arguments of those who wish to claim that the concept of class is of diminished or limited explanatory importance in sociology, a claim to which we turn in the next chapter.

Conclusion

Countries that occupy a similar niche within the world-system present us with diverse class structures and degrees of class inequality. On balance, therefore, the nation-state appears to be the most salient geographical reference for class stratification. This is not to deny the existence of world-system influences. But location in the world-system is only one element, together with welfare state policies, history, and culture, that combine to shape a nation's class structure. This leads to four conclusions. First, it is exceedingly difficult to isolate with any confidence the overall effect on class stratification of any one element, such as the nature of the political system. Second, because the various elements come together at the level of the nation-state, the nation-state has a far higher degree of distinctiveness in terms of stratification than any supra-national geographical or economic unit. Third, specific welfare state policies in areas such as education and health cause the abatement of class inequalities. This reinforces the claim of the nation-state to be the appropriate geographical unit for the study of class stratification because of the diverse ways in which states can pursue welfare state objectives that filter world-system effects. The specifics of national welfare state policies are an important and highly visible vehicle for linking class position and life chances, and are perhaps the main reason why a middle-class Briton and a middle-class Swede do not have more in common. Fourth, there are nonetheless straws in the wind that suggest that a more complex geography of class is imminent, perhaps has already arrived. The implications of that complexity have yet to be widely discussed, not least because those who study stratification typically work with data that describes class structures of the recent past, not of the present.

Notes

1. Wright, for example, finds that a common set of class-based attitudes characterize the capitalist classes but not the working classes of Sweden and the United States (1989a:37).
2. In the same volume as Wallerstein, Balibar (1991) reaches the opposite conclusion about the geographical base of class struggle: 'Thus, though the world-economy is the real battleground of the class struggle, there is no such thing as a world proletariat (except "as an idea"), indeed, it exists even less than does a world bourgeoisie' (1991:178).
3. Specificity in the form of country names exemplifying or even falling under these three labels is not very helpful, particularly in discerning the nature of the semi-periphery. For example, one of the more

empirically sophisticated attempts at classifying countries according to 'world-system status' found three semi-peripheral blocks. The block emerging as most clearly semi-peripheral was diverse indeed, encompassing Bulgaria, Cuba, Cyprus, East Germany, Hungary, Iran, Iraq, Ireland, Israel, Jordan, Lebanon, Rumania, Turkey, and the USSR (Snyder and Kick 1979). Clearly, as Weede and Kummer (1985) conclude, we are dealing with ideal types: empirically, countries are arrayed along a continuum of world-system attributes. See also the typologies in Ragin and Delacroix (1979).

4. Any summary of the world-system perspective is inevitably crude, and fails to convey the depth of historical analysis on which it is based. Our summary draws upon the classification of approaches to the international division of labour provided by Ragin and Delacroix (1979).

5. This parallels the argument of Weber's 'Last Theory of Capitalism', with a vital difference: the finely balanced struggle that provides capitalism with its underlying dynamic is for Weber the reason that the system will persist, while for Wallerstein it is the source of its ultimate and certain demise (Collins 1992). To Weber,

> The possibility for the follower-societies of the non-Western world to acquire the dynamism of industrial capitalism depends on there being a balance among class forces, and among competing political forces and cultural forces as well. In the highly industrialized societies also, the continuation of capitalism depends on continuation of the same conflicts. The victory of any one side would spell the doom of the system. (Collins 1992:98–9)

6. Chase-Dunn (1989:43) argues that class exploitation, which is rooted within national stratification systems, is the more important for the accumulation of capital, but that core/periphery exploitation is 'nevertheless essential because of its political effects on the mobility of capital and in reducing class conflict and weakening anti-capitalist movements in the core'. Core/periphery exploitation is thus basic to his definition of the capitalist mode of production, and fundamental to the stability of that system.

7. Amin (1975) is a standard reference to a substantial claim that the internationalization of class struggle is a likely outcome of trends in the world economy.

8. National ties are particularly strong for those engaged in welfare state activities. One estimate puts the welfare state (*c.* 1985) responsible for 28 per cent of employment in Denmark and 17 per cent in the United States (Rose 1985:11). An important national difference is the direct funding of that employment. In Denmark, virtually all welfare state employment is in the public sector, compared to less than half (45 per cent) in the United States (Esping-Andersen 1990:15).

9. Such East–West comparisons may however be unreliable guides to the relative distribution of life chances. Przeworski (1991:120) notes the 'bewildering' picture that emerges from indicators of welfare in such comparisons: 'Socialist countries tend to have more doctors per capita, higher high-school enrolment rates, and more construction of housing and at the same time a shorter life expectancy, a higher gross mortality, lower labour productivity, and inferior housing standards'.

10. Mobility data are available from studies conducted in Czechoslovakia, Hungary, and Poland during the 1970s, compared to similar studies in ten Western societies. A more narrowly drawn comparison – between Austria, Czechoslovakia, and Hungary – does find evidence of a distinctive state socialist mobility regime (Haller *et al.* 1990).

11. Burawoy and Lukács argue that class consciousness is a product of the regime of production present in the workplace, independent of the consciousness that workers bring to the enterprise from outside. Their *post hoc* explanation for the demise of state socialism emphasizes the dissent generated by the state socialist enterprise, combined with the influence of a dominant class drawn to the ideology of capitalism to replace one in which it no longer had faith (1992:148).

12. Haller *et al.*'s findings also highlight the transient nature of the association between national geographic boundaries and class structures, a topic that we consider later in the chapter.

13. The later point reflects what Burawoy and Krotov believe to be the greatly weakened bargaining position of management, one that accentuates the weakness inherent to state socialism. Management must resort to establishing 'cooperatives' or 'small enterprises' within the workplace with which to employ workers at higher rates for overtime (Burawoy and Krotov 1992:35).

14. The Soviet Union was perhaps distinctive in its lack of a clear and consistent plan for effecting the transition to democracy and a market economy. One of the leading reformers, and Gorbachev's chief ideologist, Aleksandr Yakovlev, defended the failure to define an alternative to capitalism to replace state socialism:

> 'But imagine what would have happened if we'd just gone into an office and created an entire scheme. Marx did that and look what it led to! One should take things from life, and adjust them every day. Our whole trouble is that we are inert, we think in dogmas. Even if reality tells us to change things, we always check first in a book'. (Remnick 1994:298)

15. And here we depart from Esping-Andersen in including both capitalist and state socialist societies.

CHALLENGES TO CLASS ANALYSIS

Introduction

Despite the centrality of class analysis to sociology (or perhaps because of it) claims have frequently been made about the demise of class as a useful sociological concept. In 1959, for example, writing in the *Pacific Sociological Review*, Robert Nisbet claimed that class 'is nearly valueless for the clarification of the data on wealth, power and social status in the contemporary United States' (Nisbet 1959:11). This is echoed in contemporary statements on both sides of the Atlantic. For example, Clark and Lipset (1991:397) argue that 'Social class was the key theme of past stratification work. Yet class is an increasingly outmoded concept.' Similarly, in Britain, Pahl's (1989:710) assertion that 'class as a concept is ceasing to do any useful work for sociology' reiterates what has been argued by a number of authors during the 1970s and 80s.

Several arguments are advanced in support of such assertions: particularly influential in Britain has been the claim that it is differences in consumption, rather than production, which are nowadays central to the formation of interest groups in society. Developments labelled under the broad heading of post-modernism have suggested that, with the apparent decline of large-scale manufacturing (encapsulated under the heading of 'Fordism') and its replacement by post-Fordist 'flexible accumulation', the social forms associated with modernism – including the idea of classes as collective actors – are no longer relevant in understanding how society is structured. They have been replaced by a more fluid, less certain structuring of social relationships, within a context in which groups undertaking collective action may form on a plethora of bases.

In this chapter we will look at some of these issues. We begin by briefly recapitulating some of the themes presented in the first chapter, notably the distinction between stratification *per se* and class stratification, our intention being to situate other forms of stratification within this broad framework. We then go on to address two questions. The first of these concerns whether or not there is evidence that class is declining in importance in either absolute terms or relative to other forms of stratification in its importance for the distribution of life chances and forms of consciousness or as a basis for the formation of social groups acting collectively.

Our second question concerns the relationship between class stratification, gender and race. In recent years a number of criticisms have been made of class analysis from what is sometimes called a 'feminist' standpoint. In particular it has been argued that class analysis fails to take account of gender stratification and that class analysis is 'gender blind' in ways that invalidate it. We will examine some of these issues. This will require that we address questions relating to whether or not the family is the appropriate unit of class composition. It also requires us to consider the nature of the relationship between class and other forms of stratification – not only gender but also race.

Stratification

In the first chapter of this book we argued that the study of stratification is concerned with the way in which characteristics of actors lead to them occupying a particular position on one or more dimensions of social power. We noted that there are multiple dimensions of social power and, furthermore, there can be different bases from which resources and constraints derive. It follows then that some bases of stratification might be considered particularly appropriate to account for the distribution of actors on one dimension of social power and not another. On the other hand, it may also be the case that different bases of stratification might be used to account for the distribution of actors on the same dimension of social power. For example, the distribution of economic resources and constraints might be argued to arise from both class and ethnic stratification. Or, a particular expression of preferences through behaviour – such as voting – might be structured both by class and age.

In the case of *class* stratification, the common characteristic shared by actors has to do with the way in which they secure their livelihood – specifically with the position they occupy in relations defined by labour markets and productive processes. Empirically the centrality of class for sociologists has rested on its claim to being a significant determinant of life chances. The purposive acts of individual actors are undertaken from a position of social power which is determined, to an important extent, by class membership. This position of social power – the resources individuals possess and the constraints they face – in turn leads to certain courses of action having a higher probability of being undertaken than others. At the same time, a particular position of social power is a powerful factor shaping perceptions and preferences, the latter supplying the motives for action. Taken together these processes lead to class position becoming a powerful predictor of many kinds of behaviour.

The decline of classes for themselves?

Similar arguments to those made above can also be advanced in respect of other bases of stratification, such as gender and ethnicity: indeed, one can hypothesize that, all other things being equal, the likelihood of specific class (or gender or ethnic) interests giving rise to collective action is inversely related to the number and salience of the bases of stratification in a given context. In simpler terms, women, for example, are less likely to recognize their collective interests and to act collectively to pursue them if they are widely distributed over class positions. The same holds true for members of an ethnic group or a class, who may be divided by, say, religion or some other factor which is itself a source of structured inequalities. If the variation that exists in life chances within a class or gender or ethnic group is itself structured in some way, then class interests are less likely to be articulated and class action is less likely to occur, not least because actors will have a variety of interests, not all of which may be compatible with their 'class interests'.

None of this is to deny the significance of class or the other bases of stratification: rather it is to make the point that the chances of class action are diminished by the extent of cross-cutting of the bases on which life chances are structured. In part, however, it has been the manifest failure of class members to act collectively in accordance with what are believed to be their class interests that has led to announcements of the decline of class as a useful sociological concept. In other words, those who proclaim the demise of class often do so because of the failure of classes to act 'for themselves' (Bauman 1982; Hindess 1987; Holton and Turner 1989; Lukes 1984; Offe 1985 among others). But these critics are, *de facto*, adopting a view of class which is at once too narrow and too broad – too broad because it implicitly assigns to classes by definition a role which is contingent, and too narrow because it sees class as only existing or only being a useful concept in the sense of a 'class for itself'. The link between class position and collective action was only ever (theoretically) unproblematic within certain Marxist theories of class:[1] for others the link between these two was, as we have seen, a matter for empirical investigation. Indeed, Max Weber believed that shared status, rather than class, was a more likely basis for the formation of social groups.

Class and political party preference

A convincing challenge to the utility of class analysis would, in our view, be one which demonstrated that class position was of much diminished utility in accounting for at least one of the following three possible outcomes of class position:

the distribution of life chances;

forms of consciousness or preferences;

forms of behaviour which had previously been linked to class (such as voting).

In Britain a good deal of attention has been paid to the relationship between political party preference and class. Here a number of authors have claimed that 'class dealignment' in party support has occurred. This has been particularly apparent in the decline of the traditional basis of Labour party support in the working classes, leading to the defeat of Labour by the Conservatives at the British General Elections of 1979, 1983, 1987 and 1992. Some of the most widely cited explanations of this apparent decline in class voting suggest that 'new sectional interests . . . reflected . . . in the growth of instrumental, pecuniary, egoistic values and attitudes' have replaced 'older forms of solidarity based on community, unionism or class itself' (Marshall 1987:38; Lukes 1984:279). An important reason for this is the increased complexity of systems of stratification:

> For the truth is that the class structure has radically changed over the last decades, becoming both more complex and more obscure; that in consequence the parties to the old Labour alliance have fragmented in various cross-cutting, ambiguous and contradictory ways. (Lukes 1984:278)

This, in turn, has occurred because (among other factors) of the internationalization of the economy, the move from industry to services which, together with changes in the nature of work has eroded the manual/non-manual distinction, and the decline in the centrality of work to personal identity. Hobsbawm (1981) focuses on the fragmenting of the working class through such changes as the growth in service and public sector employment and the increased labour force participation of women and immigrants from the New Commonwealth. For Hobsbawm the result has been the replacement of collective values by individualism, while Lukes points to new divisions that shape individual interests – between the employed and the unemployed, for example, and between those members of the working class who own property and those who do not.

Similar arguments, to the effect that differences in *consumption* patterns rather than position in the production process have become significant in shaping individual values and outlooks at the expense of class, were taken up by a number of other authors (such as Saunders 1981; Dunleavy and Husbands 1985) and appeared to receive some empirical support. Sarvlik and Crewe

(1983; also Crewe 1986) argued that since the 1960s the class bases of support for both the Conservative and Labour parties had declined, each coming to rely upon a wider constituency.

More recently, however, the empirical underpinnings of these arguments have been challenged. A number of authors (notably Gallie 1988; Marshall 1987; Marshall *et al.* 1988) have pointed out that the forms of class-based solidarity which are argued to have declined in Britain in recent years have not, in fact, been evident for some considerable time. The conclusions of authors such as Lukes that people's values are instrumental and egoistic are not at all unlike those reported in the 'Affluent Worker' studies (Goldthorpe *et al.* 1969) of car assembly-line workers in the 1960s. Here

> the new type of worker, it was argued, had a primarily instrumental orientation to work. He continued to adhere to trade unions and to support the Labour Party, but only because these were seen to be the most effective vehicles for realizing the individual's private goals as a consumer. (Gallie 1988:474)

Reanalysis of data on voting patterns has also weakened the thesis of class dealignment. Heath *et al.* (1985) showed that, although the Labour party did indeed lose working-class support over the period 1964–83, it also lost support from all other classes. In other words, while it is true that the percentage of working-class voters who voted Labour declined, so did the percentage of middle-class voters. As a result, Heath *et al.* found no trend over this period in the relative *class composition* of Labour party support.

These studies undermine the notion that working-class solidarity in Britain has somehow declined: rather, taken together with the findings of the earlier 'Affluent Worker' studies they suggest that:

> there is no evidence that the Labour Party was supported out of attachment to values of redistribution or out of any strong sense of class solidarity . . . Support for the Labour Party was based primarily on instrumental motives and hence was always vulnerable to erosion if manual workers could be persuaded that their personal economic interests lay elsewhere. (Gallie 1988:478)

None of these counter arguments, however, need imply that 'consumption cleavages' or other forms of social differentiation have no impact on voting behaviour or party support. They do, however, imply (and recent empirical evidence – such as Saunders 1990 – supports such an implication) that such sectoral cleavages are less important than class. Indeed, Hamnett (1989) makes the case that consumption patterns themselves derive, to a considerable degree, from class position. One might therefore argue that to the extent that these cleavages can indeed be shown to be related to class position they provide evidence of the mechanisms or links through which class comes to influence voting behaviour.

New forms of social organization

Arguments about the declining significance of class position for party preference are part of a larger body of literature that claims classes are becoming less important because of changes in the organization of production, and which, in some versions, goes on to suggest new bases on which life chances are structured. Perhaps the longest standing such tradition in sociology is what is sometimes called the 'liberal theory of industrialism' (Kerr *et al.* 1960; Kerr 1969; Parsons 1960, 1964, 1970; Treiman 1970). Here the argument is that the class one is born into will decline in importance as a factor influencing subsequent life chances as part of a general diminishing in the significance of ascriptive factors (gender, race, ethnicity, and so on) and their replacement by achievement-based criteria for personal advancement, notably educational and other impartially certified qualifications. These developments will occur for two main reasons: first, classes which own the means of production and in which inheritance of class position is of paramount importance for class reproduction (as in the cases of farmers and the petty bourgeoisie) will decline in number while the number of employees will increase. Second, among employees jobs will increasingly be acquired on the basis of achievement. This, it is argued, is a functional necessity of capitalism. In order to compete with other nations an economy must ensure that the optimum use is made of its population's abilities: hence the acquisition of position on the grounds of anything other than merit will be sub-optimal from the point of view of the economy's competitive position. In allocating positions on the basis of achievement, educational credentials will come to play the central role. This process is sometimes termed 'expanding universalism' (Blau and Duncan 1967:430). One consequence of the liberal theory's predictions should be a convergence of societies to one common form of 'industrial society'. This aspect of the theory is usually termed the 'convergence thesis' and it is an argument that has latterly been revived by the break-up of the formerly state socialist regimes of Central and Eastern Europe (Fukuyama 1989).

The liberal theory then predicts that class will diminish in its role as a determinant of life chances. Other authors have sought to explain how continued economic development will realign the class structure. Braverman (1974), for example, argued that a deskilling of white-collar work would lead to widespread 'proletarianization' with the deskilled white-collar workers finding common cause with traditional manual workers. Conversely, Daniel Bell's (1974) thesis was that the inexorable expansion of the white-collar middle class was part of the development of a 'post-industrial society' in which the middle classes would see their interests as increasingly distinct from those of the manual classes, being best pursued through professional and similar organizations rather than through the traditional trade unions.

All these arguments seek to extrapolate from changes in the production process to consequences for forms of social organization. More recently, post-modernist writers have sought to make the same links. Here it is argued that 'Fordism' has given way to 'flexible accumulation'. By Fordism is meant not simply a particular form of production but also a way of organizing demand (and society at large) through the development of mass consumption to match mass production, aided by the growth of welfare states, Keynesian principles of macroeconomic demand management, and corporatist arrangements. Since the 1970s, however, mass production has given way to specialized forms of production; employers have sought flexibility in their employment practices largely because the arrangements that guaranteed demand for their products have been removed with the end of Keynesianism and the decline of the welfare state. At the same time there has been an explosion of choice of lifestyles, a diminishing faith in rationality as a guiding principle, and disillusion with ideologies. The result is that old forms of consciousness, characterized by collective orientations and long-term commitment, have given way to greater individualism and the formation of more transitory interest groups based on specific and immediate issues rather than ideological conviction.

One of the most influential recent statements of this position is found in Ulrich Beck's *Risk Society* (1992). Beck argues that what he terms 'reflexive modernization' dissolves the old forms of culture and consciousness associated with outmoded social forms such as class and gender in a 'social surge of individualism' (Beck 1992:87). Individualism, according to Beck (1992:88) 'means the variation and differentiation of lifestyles and forms of life, opposing the thinking behind the traditional categories of large-group societies – which is to say, classes, estates and social stratification'. Beck does not argue that what we call inequalities in life chances have vanished: however, he claims that these are no longer significantly structured by class position: there is a 'classlessness' of social inequality. These inequalities are thus individualized as personal misfortunes. In order to cope with the world as an individual, people enter into temporary coalitions focused on specific issues and specific conditions. Beck (1992:101) calls these 'pragmatic alliances in the individual struggle for existence'.

Beck would therefore appear to be making three claims, which are also found, in various combinations, in other contemporary writings on post-modern society. First, classes no longer form a basis for collective action. Second, class no longer provides a source of common values and goals. And, third, class no longer structures social inequality – at least not to the same degree as before.

The first argument is one we have met before, and to which the same response can be invoked, to the effect that the evolution of a class in itself to a class for itself has always been considered problematic and contingent upon factors other than those directly linked to social class. It may be that such an evolution is less likely to occur today – indeed the increasingly heterogenous sources of personal identity suggest that Beck may well be correct. But this is an empirical matter that does not of itself diminish the utility of the concept of class.[2]

Similarly, Beck's second argument shares much in common with some of those we examined earlier in the context of the issue of class de-alignment – notably the assumption that, in the past, class membership provided the basis for a kind of moral consciousness or set of interests distinct from self-interest. And, for the reasons advanced by Gallie (1988) and Marshall (1987), we would do well to be sceptical of arguments which posit the existence of such a 'golden age' at some point in the past.[3]

Beck's third argument can also be subjected to empirical scrutiny and this is something we turn to in the next section.

Class and life chances

Beck's arguments suggest that class should have lost some, if not all, of its force in explaining social inequalities: similarly, the liberal theory of industrialism posits the withering away of class as a basis on which life chances are determined. Most of the empirical evidence we have, however, suggests little if any diminution in the strength of the relationship between class position and life chances. Studies of, for example, the relationship between class of origin and educational attainment in Britain during this century detect little or no change in the differential in educational advantages accruing to children from different class backgrounds, despite the substantial reforms that took place over the period (for example, Heath and Clifford 1990; Heath, Mills and Roberts 1992). Substantially the same result has emerged from studies of a range of other countries (Blossfeld and Shavit 1993). Similarly the chances of access to different destination classes as between men of different origin classes appear to have been remarkably stable over the course of this century in a number of countries (Erikson and Goldthorpe 1992b, Chapter 3).[4] Anyone who doubts the significance of class as a determinant of life chances need only consult Reid's (1989) *Social Class Differences in Britain* to find ample evidence of the pervasive effects of class across a whole range of areas. As Goldthorpe and Marshall (1992:393) state: there is 'a remarkable persistence of class-linked inequalities and of class-differentiated patterns of social action, even within periods of rapid change at the level of economic structure, social institutions and political conjunctures'.

Can we explain why the two theses we have examined and which suggest a decline in these inequalities should not have received empirical support? In the case of the liberal theory the answer is that it takes too simplistic a view of the extent to which the forces of competition between national economies will lead to changes in the processes by which individuals come to occupy their position is society. It neglects the means by which those who possess privilege can maintain it, for themselves and their family, even in the face of the 'functional requirements' of modern industrialism and the legislation that may accompany these (Breen and Whelan 1993:6).

Beck's case returns us to the model of stratification we developed in Chapter 1 and the important distinction between the sharing of a common position on one of the *bases* of social power and sharing a common position of social power. Thus it is quite possible that the degree to which the latter is structured by, among other things, class, will go unrecognized, particularly if the factors mediating between the bases of social power and positions of social power become more complex,[5] thus rendering the bases of social power less transparent. It is in this sense that we might agree with Lukes's argument that the class structure has become more obscure – but, we might add, it can become obscure to the professional sociologist no less than to the woman or man in the street.

Status attainment research

The empirical evidence does, then, we believe, suggest that class position remains a very important determinant of life chances. However, class position is, as we know, based on (to put it crudely) how a family obtains its livelihood. Might it not be possible, therefore, that the best way of capturing the position that an individual or family occupies in the structure of resources and constraints as a result of their attachment to the productive process is not through class position but through some other measure? Income is an obvious example: other possibilities are prestige or ranking on a 'socio-economic index'. This has been the focus of much American sociology in what is called 'status attainment' research.

Status attainment research originated in the work of Otis Dudley Duncan. This exemplifies a distinctly American approach to stratification in which social class structure is relegated to the margins. Stratification is, instead, expressed through a continuum of positions.[6] The American experience of, seemingly, absorbing a succession of ethnic immigrants into a vast middle-class melting pot led to a 'view of society as a benign system composed of a static hierarchical structure of positions; with individual rewards based on achieved contribution to society's needs; and legitimized by a system of universally shared values' (Grimes 1991:116). Here Marx and Weber are very distant influences, filtered almost beyond recognition through the functionalist theories summarized by the ascribed status/achieved status and particularistic/universalistic 'pattern variables' of Talcott Parsons. The triumph of achieved over ascribed status is considered a hallmark of industrial society. Class is one of many ascribed statuses, ordained at birth, that is a declining force in influencing the success in life that individuals realize. It follows that social classes are atrophied remnants of earlier, now superseded, societal forms, and therefore largely irrelevant to the contemporary study of stratification. Stratification is seen as inexorably becoming more homogenous in terms of preferences and resources: 'Objective criteria of evaluation that are universally accepted increasingly pervade all spheres of life and displace particularistic standards of diverse in-groups, intuitive judgements, and humanistic values' (Blau and Duncan 1967:429).

While Blau and Duncan, like their mentor Parsons, appreciate the continuing role of ascribed, particularistic bases of stratification in affecting life chances, they assume their impact to be diminishing and ignore their interaction with supposedly universalistic (that is, market-based) stratification processes (Matras 1975:285–6 is one of many critiques[7]).

The operationalization of the status attainment approach is quite simple. Occupations are ranked on some single vertical dimension, and research focuses on examining the factors that are believed to influence where an individual gets to on this ranking. Blau and Duncan's (1967) study is the earliest and most famous such study. They constructed what they termed a 'socio-economic index of occupational status', based on the earnings accruing to, and the level of educational attainment of men in, each occupation.[8] Using survey data they then analyzed the relationship between an individual's (in fact their sample comprised only men) current occupational status and that of his first job, of his father's job, and of his own and his father's education. So, Blau and Duncan modelled the respondent's own education as being influenced by his father's education and occupation. The status of the respondent's first job was influenced by his own education and his father's occupation; and, finally, the respondent's current job's status was modelled as being influenced by the status level of his first job, his education and his father's occupation. In this way Blau and Duncan were able to assess the relative effects of ascribed (father's education and occupational status) and achieved (own education) features in determining a person's current occupational position: put crudely they measured the effects of some of the determinants of success in the modern United States. Since then very many other similar studies have been carried out in both the United States and elsewhere, using similar rankings of occupations, including earnings (for a British example, Psacharopoulos 1977).

Rather than status attainment research being seen as a challenge to class analysis it is better viewed as a rather different undertaking. Class is a significant determinant of the things that status attainment research focuses on – namely social standing or income – and is a better measure of life chances, particularly when these include future prospects. As Hout *et al.* (1993) put it, 'The part-time school teacher, the semi-skilled factory worker, and the struggling shopkeeper may all report the same income on their tax returns, but we recognize that as salaried, hourly, and self-employed workers (respectively) they have different sources of income and, consequently, different life chances' (parentheses added).

Furthermore, class analysis retains a focus on groups: the positions that constitute a class share a commonality in their position in labour markets and the means of production. They are not simply grouped together because (at least potentially) they share more or less common life chances: rather, they share common life chances because of the shared position they occupy. Furthermore class position may be the source of common interests, values and preferences, and, under some circumstances, of collective action. By contrast, status attainment research ranks individuals on a simple hierarchy. It looks at the question of who gets where on this vertical dimension: it is not concerned with groups in any sense.

Class and race

The persistence and pervasiveness of race as a basis for social differentiation lead some theorists to question the primacy of class. Instead, they describe the United States, Britain, and other Western nations as 'race centered societies' (Van Dijk 1987). During the nineteenth-century expansion of European and American societies, race was transformed from 'a rather harmless intellectual exercise of human classification into a lethal basis of social inequalities' (Stanfield 1991:244). Social and cultural qualities became linked to physical traits, creating a new basis for social stratification within and between nations. The organization of societies and relationships among nations are thus to be viewed as primarily structured by race, not by class.

Why is race so potent a base for the distribution of social power? One answer is that race presents a special case of ethnicity:

> whenever ethnic divisions occur along class lines, there is the likelihood, or at least the potential, that ordinary class conflict will manifest itself as ethnic conflict, in reality as well as appearance.
>
> If there is an iron law of ethnicity, it is that when ethnic groups are found in a hierarchy of power, wealth and status, then conflict is inescapable. However, where there is social, economic and political parity among the constituent groups, ethnic conflict, when it occurs, tends to be at a low level and rarely spills over into violence. (Steinberg 1989:170)

But when race forms the ethnic divide, the result is more resilient because of the propensity of people to associate race with the presence of social stigma.

The largest accumulation of theoretical and empirical work on race and stratification refers to the United States. Certainly, race rather than class dominates public policy debate in the United States, and racial rather than class labels are the common currency of street-level social stratification. People talk about race and ethnicity. Class, as Scase (1992) notes, has urgency today only among social scientists.

However, the empirical question of whether race or class is the more important principle of stratification in the United States remains unresolved (Thomas 1993:329). Some argue that 'race and class are competing modalities by which social actors may be organized', and that race is the dominant base of social power, determining class relationships and class identities (Omi and Winant 1994:32).

In our view the issue is more adequately stated in terms of how class and race are interrelated. Three main lines of argument currently compete for influence among American social scientists.[9] One argument minimizes the influence of class, arguing instead that institutional discrimination applies with equal force across all classes and limits the life chances of all blacks. So a class-by-class comparison of whites and African-Americans will find that in each class race matters and matters significantly.

A second argument offers a different, almost opposite, assessment. Race is declining in significance for the life chances of African-Americans, a view most influentially stated by William J. Wilson (1978; 1987). In this interpretation, the mid-1960s represents a watershed, in which stratification by race gave way to class stratification. By ending segregation, civil rights legislation brought African-Americans for the first time into the national economy and thus into the class structure. Within a given social class, races experience similar life chances. Thus, 'the problems of blacks are due to their over-representation in the lower class . . . Racial effects are, therefore, a function of social class and class-related phenomena, such as the prevalence of female-headed families, lack of marketable skills, and the suburbanization of industry and jobs' (Thomas 1993).

This is a classic statement of the underclass argument, as outlined in Chapter 4.[10] Economic emancipation coincided with changes in the global and national economies that, literally, moved the more attractive employment opportunities beyond the reach of much of Black America. Those with the training and qualifications to take advantage of positions within the national class structure formed a small black middle class that moved out of the traditional ghetto communities.[11] This exacerbated the effects of the unemployment and underemployment of black males for those families that remained.

Wilson offers an elegant formulation of the interplay between class and race in contemporary America. Elegance is perhaps achieved by a lack of attention to nuance. For example, Wilson's approach tends to ignore or downplay both the extent of pre-1960s class divisions within the black community (Sugrue 1993:114) and the degree to which racial discrimination is being experienced in access to entry level 'service industry' occupations that objectively require minimal educational qualifications (Steinberg, 1989:289–90). More generally, the clarity and completeness of the changes effected during the mid-1960s have been questioned (Omi and Winant 1994:27–9).

Wilson (1991) has responded to these and other criticisms by advocating an approach in which the change from race to class-based stratification is equally rooted in the national economy and in the specific constraints of living in a ghetto. The concept that spans those levels is 'weak labour-force attachment', which is Wilson's explanation for why some groups are more vulnerable than others to joblessness:

> weak labour-force attachment refers to the marginal economic position of some people in the labour-force because of structural constraints or limited opportunities, including constraints or opportunities in their immediate environment – for example, lack of access to informal job networks systems. The key theoretical distinction I am trying to make here is that there are two major sources of weak labour-force attachment – one derives from macro-structural changes in the broader society, most notably the economy, the other from the individual's social milieu. (Wilson 1991: 9–10)

This clarifies the relationship between class and racial stratification because the urban ghetto is the milieu primarily of African-Americans. Most of the poor, regardless of race or ethnicity, do not live in ghettos. But the composition of America's ghetto communities is racially and ethnically skewed: in 1980 21 per cent of black poor and 16 per cent of Hispanic poor lived in ghettos, compared to 2 per cent of the non-Hispanic white poor. When the focus is restricted to the urban poor, one-third of poor blacks living in metropolitan areas live in ghettos (Jargowsky and Bane, cited in Wilson 1991:2).[12]

This gives concrete expression to the way in which race and class intersect in the concept of an underclass – or, as Wilson now prefers, the 'ghetto poor':

> The concept 'underclass' or 'ghetto poor' can be theoretically applied to all racial and ethnic groups, and to different societies if the conditions specified in the theory are met. In studies in the United States, the concept will more often refer to minorities

because the white poor seldom live in ghettos or extreme urban poverty areas. (Wilson 1991:12)

Ultimately, then, the meaning of the underclass, and its capacity to untangle the relationship between race and class, will vary with the nation-state. It is an empirical issue. As such, Wilson concludes that class stratification has primacy in the contemporary United States.

Yet a third perspective focuses on the interaction between race and class, in which the social power associated with race varies depending on one's class. Here, two specifications of that interaction are influential. One focuses on the middle-class, arguing that African-Americans who fall within the middle-class ambit are closed out of positions of power within organizations through discrimination and white resistance. Working-class whites and non-whites are viewed as experiencing roughly similar life chances.

The other strand sees the interaction as taking place between race and working-class membership. While middle-class whites and blacks enjoy broadly similar life chances, in the working-class blacks are disadvantaged because they experience greater discrimination and lack of the resources to counter that discrimination. Moreover, the boost that affirmative action and other programmes provides to middle-class blacks is not available to the black working class because they lack the resources to take advantage of such public policy initiatives. Such a view, however, runs counter to the evidence of substantial racial and ethnic income disparities among college graduates, disparities consistently in favour of whites. Perhaps the most telling indication is the low average incomes, relative to that earned by whites, of Asians in the United States, the group held up as contemporary beneficiaries of the 'American Dream'. Reviewing the evidence, Jencks (1993:39–40) concludes:

> Chinese and Japanese Americans have generally attended good schools, do very well on standardized tests, and live in affluent parts of the country. Almost all observers . . . describe them as hardworking and highly motivated. There is no obvious explanation for their low earnings other than discrimination.

The impact of racial discrimination appears to cut across class divisions.

There is, however, no definitive test that can tell us which perspective most accurately explains the current relationship between race and class in the United States or elsewhere. For example, Steinberg (1989:291) argues that 'class disabilities are real enough, but they are the byproduct of past racism, they are reinforced by present racism, and they constitute the basis for perpetuating racial divisions and racial inequalities'. Simply put, the distinctions that constitute a national class structure represent both economic and ethnic bases of social power. It follows that a comparison of the relative importance of class and race is artificial.

Our preference for treating class as the primary basis for social stratification rests on the criteria stated earlier in this chapter. Burawoy (1985:9) offers a succinct, but less empirically driven, argument along similar lines:

> While gender and racial domination may have a greater tenacity than class domination, class is the more basic principle of organization of contemporary society. This means two things. First, class better explains the development and reproduction of contemporary societies. Second, racial and gender domination are shaped by the class in which they are embedded more than forms of class domination are shaped by gender and race.

We can with some confidence adopt such a stance in connection with the way in which stratification by race (or ethnicity) comports with class analysis. Parkin, here, points the way with the concepts of social closure: usurpation and exclusion. On balance, therefore, the interrelationship between race and class can be expressed within existing theories of class stratification. Current debates concerning the relationship between class and gender, however, challenge some of the fundamental premises through which class analysis is conducted.

Class and gender

In recent years class analysis, in what we might call its traditional form, has come under attack on a number of counts concerning the position of women (for an early example see Acker 1973). Critics have pointed, for example, to the dearth of studies of the class mobility of women. However, many of the critiques go beyond such empirical points to challenge more fundamental elements of class analysis. In this section, we look at two such challenges to class analysis, the first concerning the appropriate unit of class analysis, the second concerning the relationship between class classifications and gender.

The unit of class composition

In Chapter 1, we outlined the 'conventional' view of class analysis (Goldthorpe 1983). This is characterized by two features: first, the appropriate unit of class analysis is the family, not the individual, and, second, the class position of the family derives from the position occupied by the male head of household in labour markets and/or production units.[13] The 'dominance approach' retains the first of these features, but modifies the second such that it is the position of the partner with the dominant 'work situation' that determines the family's class. As we noted, in practice these two approaches give very similar results since the man's occupation dominates the woman's in most cases.

Critiques of these approaches have focused on both elements. There are those who, like Heath and Britten (1984) retain the household based on the conjugal family as the appropriate unit of class analysis, but seek to incorporate the wife's position as a determinant of the family's class. Other authors reject the family as the unit of class analysis and seek to assign individuals to classes.

The idea of the household as the appropriate unit of class analysis is 'commonly found among theorists of class from Schumpeter . . . through to Parkin' (Erikson and Goldthorpe 1992b:233). One obvious reason why this is the case is that the members of a family[14] usually enjoy some commonality in their material conditions and prospects. So, if the individual from whom the class position of the family is derived experiences 'upward' class mobility, the rewards that accrue will, in most cases, affect not simply that individual but the members of his or her family or household also. This is not to argue that all family members necessarily enjoy an equal share in the family's income, wealth or status or that they enjoy equal power and autonomy in making decisions concerning the family. However, their prospects and life chances are ultimately limited by the class position they enjoy by virtue of their family membership. The situation here is analogous to that described earlier in the relationship between class and other forms of stratification. Just as there exists stratification on the basis of, say, gender, age or ethnicity within a class, so there exist inequalities within families. Thus, the life chances of a particular individual are shaped both by (*inter alia*) his or her class position and the position occupied within the family. The analysis of relationships within a family is, on this account, a different undertaking from class analysis. The commonly subordinate position of women in the family is thus not an issue for class analysis *per se*, and the use of the dominant (usually male) partner's position to classify the family reflects the reality of the subordinate position which women continue to occupy within the family.

Erikson and Goldthorpe (1992b:234) have suggested that the case for the individual, as opposed to the family, as the appropriate unit of class composition, is difficult to find, even in the writings of those (like Stanworth 1984; Walby 1986; Abbot and Sapsford 1987) who have advocated this approach. In part this reflects some fundamental conceptual differences about the proper scope of class analysis, and this is an issue we shall turn to later. However, the argument made by Stanworth, for example, might be summarized as claiming that women's paid work outside the household has important effects on things like family income, provisions for old age, children's education and the like (1984:162) and thus should not be ignored, despite the fact that the woman's work might be of less importance than the man's. However, this is not really so much an argument for the individual as the unit of class composition as it is for the assignment of families to classes on the basis of both men's and women's paid employment. An argument for the individual as the unit of class analysis would have to rest on the empirical result that, in cases where the individual's class position differed from that of his or her family, the former was a more important source than the latter of some or all of life chances, preferences and potential collective identity. Proponents of the 'individual' approach to class composition have shown that women's class 'makes a difference' to a family's position but they have not demonstrated its *greater* importance in situations in which the family's class is different – which is what would seem to be required. So (to borrow an example from Erikson and Goldthorpe 1992b:236–7), one consequence of the individual approach to class composition would be that two women shop assistants, one married to an unskilled manual worker, the other to a business manager, would belong to the same class. But, in practice, two such women would enjoy very widely differing conditions of life (among other things) as a result of their husbands' positions. And, to extend the example, these two women should (according to the individual approach) enjoy a greater similarity in life chances than, say, two women, both married to unskilled manual workers but one of whom is a shop assistant while the other is a supervisor on an assembly line. Such anomalies suggest that the individual approach to the unit of class composition entails some very undesirable consequences.

A number of empirical analyses, using data from several countries, also give little support to the individual approach, especially where this entails assigning women to a class different from that of their husband. These studies show that the class position of a woman's husband is a better predictor than is her own class, of her situation on a range of consequences of class position (see, for Ireland, Breen and Whelan 1994; for Britain, Marshall *et al.* 1988; and for a number of European countries, Erikson and Goldthorpe 1992a). The consequences include the chances of being in poverty; subjective class identification;[15] and voting intentions. Perhaps even more striking are studies by Arber (1989, 1993) which show that the health of married women shows more variation according to their husband's class position than according to their own.

If the household or family is retained as the appropriate unit of class composition, the question then shifts to how a family's class should be determined. In those cases in which more than one partner is engaged in paid employment outside the home, is it to be determined on the basis of the work done by one such family member (as in the conventional and dominance approaches: we will call this single-person class assignment) or by both (multiple-person assignment)? The argument against the former approach is that neglecting the woman's (or the non-dominant partner's) position, transforms an ' "inferior" work force history into one that is, for purposes of class analysis, discounted' (Stanworth

1984:162). The argument for the latter approach is an empirical one: namely that the work of the non-dominant partner makes a difference to the family in ways suggested by Stanworth and others.[16]

Defenders of single-person assignment do not dispute such findings, but they do not view them as an argument for some form of multiple-person assignment of family class position. Rather, they emphasize the degree to which women's paid work remains, to a very large degree, of a different form to men's. As McRae (1990:122) has noted, the challenge to the conventional approach to class composition came about because of the increased labour force participation of married women. Defenders of single-person assignment, however, draw on arguments that suggest that this increased participation is of a very partial kind. For example, almost half of total female employment in the United Kingdom is part-time, women's work histories continue to be intermittent (being interrupted by childbirth and childrearing), and their earnings are lower than those of men. It is considerations such as these that led Hakim (1992:144) to conclude that 'the increase in women's employment since World War II is revealed to be largely illusory.' On this basis, then, Erikson and Goldthorpe (1992b:238) argue that any attempt to assign families to classes using both husband's and wife's class position is likely to be unduly affected by family life-cycle effects (whether or not the wife is working at a given point in time) and rates of class mobility are likely to be vastly inflated if the family's class changes not only each time one or other partner changes class position, but also whenever one partner (usually the wife) moves in or out of the labour force.

On this account, then, the family is to be assigned a class position on the basis of the position of that partner who has a relatively enduring attachment to the labour force. The fact that, even today, this is almost always the husband, is taken as an indication of women's continued inferior position, which the increase in female participation rates masks but has not fundamentally altered. However, there is no presumption that this will always be the case. The issue is an empirical one, and it is not difficult to envisage the circumstances under which women's labour force participation might be such as to necessitate a move to some form of joint classification of a family's class position, or under which the application of the dominance approach might lead to many more families being assigned to a class on the basis of the woman's occupation.

The scope of class analysis

Disputes of the kind we have been describing, however, presuppose agreement as to what class analysis is about: namely that it concerns the consequences of the occupation of particular positions in the productive process and/or labour markets. However, not all authors accept this. For example, 'I would argue that it is the lack of incorporation into class analysis of the structured positions associated with (the) . . . domestic division of labour that is the major flaw of the conventional approach' (Walby 1986:27, parentheses added).

To extend class analysis in this way would bring domestic labour (mainly performed by 'housewives') within its ambit.[17] Unfortunately Walby never makes it clear why class analysis should be extended to incorporate the issue of gender inequality[18] – or, more particularly, what the benefits of this approach might be over one which recognized class and patriarchy as different dimensions of stratification. One might equally well suggest that class theory should incorporate other bases of stratification, such as religion or age – but there would seem to be little to be gained from this. However, while it might seem that it is simply a matter of choice how one defines class and thus how narrowly or otherwise one sets the parameters of what it seeks to explain, these alternatives will have empirical consequences that one might hope to test in much the same way that the individual versus the family approach to class assignment has been tested. For example, is the position of men and women in various respects better accounted for in terms of their class position together with their gender position or in terms of some new definition of 'class' which incorporates both? In the absence of any such tests, the position we adopt concurs with that of Breen and Whelan (1994:3):

> The extent of class related socio-cultural variation is an empirical issue, as is the scale of such differences in comparison to those arising from other sources of differentiation within and between families. It is because class is defined in terms of employment

relationships that issues such as the relative importance of class *vis-à-vis* other influences, such as life-cycle, become matters of legitimate enquiry.

Gender, temporal change, and the structure of employment

Another argument which has been made against class analysis concerns the identification of the positions that go to make up a class. Crompton (1993:188), for example, argues that it is empirically impossible to identify class:

> independently of other processes, such as work context, organizational size and sector, cultural stereotyping, and the segmentation of the labour force by gender, ethnicity and age, which also structure both the kinds of work people do and the *de facto* nature of their employment relationships.

Arguments such as this in fact have more force in respect of some definitions of class than others. For instance, if we recall Weber's definition of classes as based on the resources that people bring to capitalist (primarily labour) markets, then it is clear that the resources he considered – property, credentials/skills and labour power – are but a subset of those which are relevant. Labour markets comprise employers and job seekers seeking to maximize their own 'utility' subject to legal and other constraints. Thus, it does not follow that the resources people bring to these markets are limited to those listed by Weber: since employers often want to discriminate on other grounds, then other 'resources' are often important – such as gender or race.[19] So, we might still view classes as market segments, but recognizing that this segmentation is, in fact, much more complicated than Weber's formulation suggests, with the resources that he considered being cross-cut by the effects of gender, ethnic, and other forms of discrimination. In such cases it would be impossible to identify class independently of these other factors – indeed, 'class', on this account, would be an amalgam of these factors.

On the other hand, such arguments have much less impact on definitions of class like those adopted by Wright and Goldthorpe. As we wrote in Chapter 1, in such schemes classes are identified with aggregates of occupations having one or more characteristics in common. So, in Goldthorpe's earlier (1980/87) writings it is common work and market situation[20] that are used to group jobs into classes. The fact that the structure of employment is shaped by gender, ethnicity, age, and so on (so that, for example, there exists ethnic segregation in employment) is not relevant when this approach is adopted: indeed, any number of factors influence the shape of the occupational structure. One can think of, for example, the degree of direct government public sector job creation or the kind of industrial development policy pursued (encouraging of native industry or attempts to attract multi-national corporations are two possibilities). Chance events might also be added to this list. As we have noted earlier, class analysis is less concerned with the factors that shape the occupational structure than with elucidating the consequences of class position and, if possible, demonstrating the nature of the link between such consequences and the criteria that are used (such as work and market situation) to form classes.[21]

A not dissimilar issue arises in discussions concerning the changing nature of various sorts of work. We have already mentioned Braverman's (1974) 'de-skilling' thesis. Clearly if his arguments are correct, it would appear that studies of social mobility are deeply flawed by virtue of the fact that the meaning of white-collar work is not the same for many men in the current occupational distribution as it was for their fathers. However, things are not so simple. The real questions, from the point of view of class, are, first, whether that characteristic of an occupation on the basis of which it is assigned to a class, has changed and, second, if so, whether this change is such as to necessitate the allocation of that occupation to a different class. So, if this characteristic is, say, work situation, we need to ask whether this aspect of the occupation has changed over time, and, if it has, whether or not this is a change that should cause us to assign the occupation to another class, or whether it simply shifts the position of that occupation relative to other occupations within the same class (see Goldthorpe 1980:122). Writing of Britain, Gallie notes that the work of Marshall *et al.* (1988), 'provides very little support for the view that there has been a sharp deterioration in the work situation of routine white collar workers or for the argument that their employment conditions have become assimilated to those of manual workers'(Gallie 1988:482). On this basis, then, while we might accept that some aspects of white-collar work may have changed, those which concern the class allocation of white-collar jobs appear to have remained unchanged – or, at the very least, to have remained sufficiently constant not to necessitate any alteration in the class allocation of such jobs.

Conclusions

This chapter has examined some challenges to analyses based on the idea of class. The idea that class is of declining significance to sociology is a long-standing one: we have argued, however, that in its recent forms it receives little empirical support. As Crompton (1993:120) writes: 'the work individuals do remains the most significant determinant of the life-fates of the majority of individuals and families in advanced industrial societies.'

The relationship between class and gender, and particularly the 'feminist critiques' of class analyses were also examined. In our view the arguments for the individual, and against the family, as the unit of class composition, are not convincing – not least because retaining the family as the unit of class composition allows us to examine the effects of, say, life cycle, or of gender or ethnic stratification, independently of those of class. Furthermore, it would seem that, empirically, the assignment of families to classes is best done on the basis of the dominance approach.

None of this, however, is meant to suggest that nothing has changed or that nothing can change. For example, the arguments of writers like Beck (1992) that the bases of interest group formation have shifted towards a multiplicity of short-term alliances, do suggest that classes may be less likely to play a role as collective actors. However, such a change is, at most, one of degree, rather than of kind.

Other changes present other difficulties for class analysis. For example, the declining rate of labour force participation by adult men is one potential source of problems as is the growth of an underclass detached from the system of production in which the defining characteristics of class, as conventionally understood, are located. To our minds, however, the strongest conclusion to emerge from this assessment of challenges to class analysis is the robustness of class, as understood in the work of writers like Wright and Goldthorpe, as a useful and valid concept in socio-logical research. There is little doubt in our minds that in the most recent debates about the 'death of class' the proponents of class analysis (for example Marshall 1991; Goldthorpe and Marshall 1992; Hout *et al.* 1993) have mounted much the more convincing arguments.

Notes

1. This link is well summarized by Pahl (1989:710–11) in terms of the movement from structure (shared material and existential circum-stances of people) through consciousness (a common awareness by people sharing such a position of their exploitation and disadvantage) to action (political or violent action leading to changes which remove the material conditions which triggered the sequence).
2. Except, of course, for those who *define* classes as so-called 'collective actors'.
3. As Marshall *et al.* (1988:206) put it: 'a communitarian and solidaristic proletariat of some bygone heyday of class antagonism is set against the atomised consumer-oriented working class of today.'
4. Although the bulk of the evidence indicates that the diminution in the strength of class relationships predicted by the liberal theory has not taken place, there are a few studies which find otherwise. Notable among these is the large cross-national study by Ganzeboom, Luijkx and Treiman (1989).
5. And if the various bases of social power come to interact in complex ways which may not diminish their effects but may make them less easily isolated.
6. The 'classic' exposition of this view is Blau and Duncan 1967. The attainment model, most closely associated with the University of Wisconsin (ironically also the 'ancestral home' of Wright's analytical Marxism) continues to be widely practised in the United States, although its predominance in the sociology journals waned in the 1970s and shows no sign of renewal.
7. We cite Matras because of his related point that Blau and Duncan's assessment of the dominance of universalism is in part an artifact of the dominance of the sample survey in social science methodology in the 1960s: random surveys of the population bring with them assumptions that:

the behaviour of one individual studied (e.g. his choice of occupation, educational aspirations or attainment, political participation, etc.) is largely independent of that of other persons in the same population . . . This may be true in a general way. But if the i-th person and j-th person are cousins, or if they migrated to the metropolis from the same rural village, and if the behaviour in question is occupational behaviour, chances are that their respective moves are not only correlated but often actually causally related. (Matras 1975:286)

8. The scale is, in fact, an attempt to capture the 'prestige' of each occupation: see Blau and Duncan 1967:119,125.
9. The threefold classification of perspectives on race and class, and the distinction between working-class and middle-class variations for the interactionist perspective, are derived from Thomas (1993). A more detailed typology is offered by Omi and Winant (1994; Chapters 1–3).
10. The term is sufficiently emotive, and has been applied to such a vast array of phenomena, that its prime advocate now argues for its abandonment (Wilson 1991) and replacement by the term 'ghetto poor'. This seems premature. A more precisely defined underclass seems essential for understanding the concentrated long-term unemployment in Western Europe and the interaction between class and status group membership in that setting.
11. Prior to mid-1960s the black middle class was based in the ghetto, rather than the national, economy. The classic study is Frazier 1957.
12. An alternative approach to describing the underclass is that 59 per cent of residents of underclass areas are black and 10 per cent Hispanic (Rickets and Sawhill, cited in Steinberg 1989:282).
13. In this discussion we frequently refer to 'husbands' and 'wives', but these terms should be taken as abbreviations for male and female partner, respectively, in a relatively enduring cohabiting relationship.
14. By 'family' we here mean individuals within a household who live together and share a more or less common pool of resources.
15. As Erikson and Goldthorpe (1992b:251) note, one implication of this result is that a woman whose own class (when assigned on an individual basis) is working class, is more likely to consider herself middle class if she is married to a man whose class position is, indeed, middle class. In order to explain why such women do not consider themselves to be working class, the proponents of the individual approach are obliged to resort to arguments about 'false consciousness'.
16. For example, Heath and Britten (1984) and Hayes and Jones (1992) demonstrate its effect on political party allegiance.
17. So, 'housewives and husbands are two classes in a patriarchal system' (Walby 1986:36).

18. Except insofar as she confuses class stratification with stratification in general.
19. See Giddens 1973:112, who considers a similar possibility when he writes of the circumstances in which 'status group membership itself becomes a form of market capacity'.
20. Though, as we have noted, in his later work with Erikson (Erikson and Goldthorpe 1992b) these criteria are modified and the emphasis is placed on employment relations that exist between positions.
21. And, in examining class mobility, factors other than class origins play a part. For example, the class mobility of men and women is influenced by the nature of gender differentiation in the occupational structure.

CHAPTER 8

CLASS AND SOCIAL POWER

Introduction

Chapter 1 presented a view of stratification as the study of the bases on which social power is distributed. By social power we mean the position occupied with respect to the resources individuals possess to enable them to undertake actions and the set of objective constraints they face in doing so. There are, of course, innumerable actions that people might seek to undertake, but in the study of stratification we concentrate on only some of these. Of particular importance are those that concern people's life chances. The distribution of individuals on the dimension of social power relating to life chances is influenced by a number of factors – such as gender and race – but the primary basis of this dimension of stratification is social class. In other words, class position is the major basis on which life chances are distributed.

Two contemporary theorists provide perspectives that mesh particularly well with our view of stratification. John Goldthorpe and Erik Olin Wright both offer sophisticated frameworks for conducting class analysis that have been implemented in extensive and comparative research programmes. Both exemplify a tradition of research in which the first step is the specification of a class structure and the allocation of individuals into class positions. This contrasts with the approach taken by Michael Burawoy, for example, who views class as a subjectively constituted phenomenon.

A quotation from Wright (1985:144) succinctly states what class analysis is all about:

Class location is a basic determinant of the matrix of objective possibilities people face in making decisions. At one level this concerns what Weber referred to as the individual's 'life chances', the overall trajectory of possibilities individuals face over the life cycle. In a more mundane way, it concerns the daily choices people face about what to do and how to do it.

Because class forms a basis for the allocation of objective resources and constraints it shapes 'the underlying capacities to act of social actors' (Pawson 1989:189). Moving from capacities to action itself, however, requires that we attend to individuals' subjective perception of objective conditions and also the preferences that they hold. Variation in these is less obviously structured than are objective resources and constraints. Nevertheless, class position plays a significant role in shaping individual preferences and perceptions. Bourdieu (1977:77), for example, indicates that one way in which class position and preferences may be interrelated is through the adaptation of preferences to the objective constraints that individuals face.[1]

Both Goldthorpe and Wright provide viable frameworks for pursuing these issues. The fundamental differences in their underlying conceptual models, however, are evident in the allocation of persons into class positions and the pictures of class structure that result from the application of their respective class schemata (see Chapters 3 and 4). This stems from theoretical differences that cannot be bridged. What separates Wright from Goldthorpe ultimately is his political allegiance to a Marxist project that:

> has to rest on a commitment to the theoretical constraints that Marxist theory imposes on class analysis. More specifically, unless one sees the value of embedding the concept of class structure in an abstract model of modes of production in which classes are fundamentally polarized around processes of exploitation, then there would be no reason to accept the difficulties this abstract framework generates for the concrete analysis of classes. (Wright 1989b:319)

This contrasts with the view that 'class analysis does not entail a commitment to any particular theory of class but, rather, to a research programme' (Goldthorpe and Marshall 1992:382). For Goldthorpe the chief criterion for the choice of one class schema over another is its greater adequacy for empirical analyses, while for Wright this is emphatically not the case.

Such differences make our choice between Goldthorpe and Wright easy. Goldthorpe's class structure meets our theoretical criteria because the distribution of social power within advanced societies conforms more closely to the categories that it, rather than Wright's schemata, distinguishes.

Unresolved issues

The class structure according to Goldthorpe seems the best of those on offer to apply to the advanced societies. Whether the same set of class categories will prove equally appropriate for nations outside the core is unclear. Intensive class analysis has been restricted to the core nations and a few from the semi-periphery with traditions of Anglo-American social science. In looking ahead to an agenda for class analysis, therefore, a logical starting point is to extend the base upon which we draw in making assertions concerning class boundaries and class structuration. This will entail a research strategy that systematically seeks to represent the diverse positions within the world-system and regions. In particular, examination of stratification patterns in countries without extensive welfare state provisions might provide clearer evidence of an association between a nation's stratification system and its position within the hierarchy of nations.

Extending the breadth of cases on which we can draw to test comparative propositions might also be valuable for inquiry into the link between ethnic and class stratification. Positions in the class structure are, after all, filled by people who differ in their gender, race, and ethnicity. The implications of this can plausibly be argued to have consequences at the macro, societal level, as well as for the fate of the individuals concerned. As Parkin (1979:4–5) notes: 'Societies marked by conflict between religious or racial communities do not exhibit the same type of class structure as societies lacking such conflict, notwithstanding similarities in their occupation systems and property relations.' Such a claim is difficult to assess at present. The evidence from stratification research in the United States, for example, is inconclusive on whether class or race has primacy in determining income levels (see Chapter 7). Welfare state provisions and labour market regulations in the United States and other ethnically diverse countries included thus far in comparative stratification blunt the differentiation of life chances according to ethnic background. A wider research net might offer a way to address more adequately the issues raised by Parkin.

The relationship between class and ethnic stratification is also likely to become more significant within the countries of central Europe. Immigration and large-scale movements of peoples as political boundaries are redrawn (as in the reunified Germany and the fragmentation of the former Yugoslavia and Czechoslovakia) highlight ethnic heterogeneity.

The way in which class analysis has dealt with the issue of gender is already being challenged by changing forms of production. To the degree that the traditional division of labour within households disappears, then there are implications for both the shape of the class structure and more generally the ways in which households are linked to that structure.

Rising female labour force participation tends to be concentrated in the lower service class and routine non-manual class. The resulting expansion of the relative size of those classes is then enhanced by the demand for more workers to serve as substitute sources of child-care and housekeeping among those families in which both spouses are in full-time employment. Such positions tend to be filled predominantly by female workers (Esping-Andersen 1993:17–18). This is a general trend. The precise impact that an influx of female employees has on the class structure will be mediated through state policies. In one country, state social services will expand to accommodate a new cadre of semi-professional employees, while in another country, the response will be a growth in the ranks of self-employed workers located at the margins of the legitimate economy.

The 'conventional' view of the relationship between households and the class structure sees the head of household's class location as being transmitted to her, or, more usually, his household. Such changes, however, present a challenge to this approach insofar as the difference between male and female partners in their attachment to the labour market diminishes. This may arise through women's labour force participation approximating ever more closely to the traditional male pattern. Equally, both genders may come to have more fragmented employment during the course of their working lives. The most likely outcome merges both these possibilities but locates them at different places in the class structure. Consider, for example, a husband and wife, both of whom are in the service class, and who work virtually without interruption (except for short periods for childbirth) throughout their working lives. Compare them to a husband and wife in the routine non-manual or non-skilled manual classes, whose periods of employment are sporadic. The consequences of this for income inequality between households would be dramatic indeed. Similarly the social mobility chances of their respective children would, in all probability, also be quite different. Further, the magnitude of such effects will be all the greater if, as seems likely, they take place during a period of welfare state retrenchment.

A final unresolved issue arises out of the growth in numbers of households in the population whose attachment to employment is not even fragmentary: in other words, households in which the potential wage earners are long-term unemployed or otherwise excluded from full participation in the labour market. To date empirical analyses have successfully rebutted the requirement to treat the unemployed as a separate class (for example, Goldthorpe and Payne 1986); furthermore, since unemployment rates vary by class, long-term unemployment might equally be viewed as a consequence of class position, conventionally defined, rather than a class position in itself. In other cases, as we noted in Chapter 4, the long-term unemployed are simply omitted from class analyses. But under current, and probable future, circumstances, none of these are satisfactory ways to address this issue. As we also in noted in Chapter 4, it has been argued that the social division between those who have jobs and those who have not has now become more significant than that based on ownership or otherwise of the means of production (Van Parijs 1989; also Offe 1985). Integrating households characterized by prolonged unemployment into its programme, in both theoretical and empirical terms, clearly provides an important challenge to class analysis.

The primacy of class

As Scase (1992:1) observes:

> Whereas sociologists will often, first and foremost, describe identities, interpersonal relationships, and social institutions by reference

to social class, this is usually not the case for the non-specialist lay person. The latter is more likely to refer to personal descriptions in terms of such factors as age, gender, occupation, ethnicity, family and place of residence.

The relative unimportance of class in lay persons' accounts of their world does not trouble us. Class is a theoretical concept which sociologists employ in order to interpret, understand, and explain the world and as such it differs from the everyday usage of the term. When sociologists explain some event or act in terms of social class they are providing an account that is of a different status from that of actors' explanations. The purpose of class analysis is not to recycle conventional wisdom; rather, 'the term "class" can act as part of a basic conceptual map of society' (Pawson 1989:254).

Students are usually told that sociology is the study of social groups. In this book we have sought to give an account of social class based on a model of stratification that begins with the behaviour of individuals. In our view, that is the most useful way to realize the potential of class to explain the distribution of power in contemporary society. A class is made up of positions in the process of production. By virtue of occupying the positions that comprise a class a set of people share a significant degree of commonality in the resources they possess and the constraints they face in undertaking actions which shape their life chances. The members of a class are therefore a group when viewed from the perspective of the sociologist. Whether they consider themselves to be a group is irrelevant to our recognition of them as a class: if they do recognize themselves as constituting a class with its own interests then we can say that they constitute a class for themselves as well as a class in themselves.

It is unusual to find a textbook which explicitly approaches the study of social class from such a perspective: nevertheless it accords well with the later approach of Erik Olin Wright, whose model is derived from game theory (as used in the analytical Marxism of John Roemer), which is a way of modelling interactions between individuals. It is perhaps even more closely linked to the methodological individualism espoused by John Goldthorpe (Erikson and Goldthorpe 1992b:1).

Books on social class tend nowadays to end with the question of whether class has a future in our post-Fordist, post-industrial, post-modern age. To us, the question is rather naive given the weight of evidence that has been accumulated in previous chapters. We have reported research from a broad, if not massive, range of countries in which the 'class principle' is deeply embedded and where the life chances of persons born this year will be strongly influenced by their class of origin. This influence extends from life expectancy to educational attainment to the prospects for a comfortable old age. Between countries and over coming decades the degree of class structuration will doubtless continue to vary. However, the strong link now established between stratification systems and the distinctive characteristics of individual nation-states seems to us a secure anchor for class-based inequalities. This does not diminish the significance or consequences associated with other forms of stratification. Nevertheless, class stratification is the dimension of social power that most directly translates differentiation in the process of production into unequal life chances. Class thus has a compelling claim to continued primacy in the study of stratification.

Note

1. But this whole area – namely the study of what is called 'endogenous preference formation' – consists of many difficult issues and few generally applicable insights.

REFERENCES

Abbot, P. and G. Payne, 1990, 'Women's Social Mobility: The Conventional Wisdom Reconsidered', in G. Payne and P. Abbot (eds) *The Social Mobility of Women*, London: Falmer Press.

Abbott, P. and R. Sapsford, 1987, *Women and Social Class*, London: Tavistock.

Abercrombie, N. and J. Urry, 1983, *Capital, Labour, and the Middle Classes*, London: Allen and Unwin.

Acker, J. 1973, 'Women and Social Stratification: A Case of Intellectual Sexism', *American Journal of Sociology*, 78, 4: 936–45.

Agnew, John A. 1987, *Place and Politics: The Geographical Mediation of State and Society*, Boston, Mass.: Allen and Unwin.

Allmendinger, J. 1989, *Career Mobility Dynamics: A Comparative Analysis of the United States, Norway and West Germany*, Berlin: Max Planck Institut für Bildungsforschung.

Amin, Shamir 1975, *Unequal Development*, New York: Monthly Review Press.

Arber S. 1989, 'Gender and Class Inequalities in Health: Understanding the Differentials', in J. Fox (ed.) *Health Inequalities in European Countries*, Aldershot: Gower.

Arber, S. 1993, 'Inequalities Within the Household', in D. Morgan and L. Stanley (eds) *Debates in Sociology*, Manchester: Manchester University Press.

Bairoch, P. 1981, 'The Main Trends in National Economic Disparities since the Industrial Revolution', in P. Bairoch and M. Levy-Leboyer (eds) *Disparities in Economic Development since the Industrial Revolution*, London: Macmillan.

Balibar, Etienne 1991, 'From Class Struggle to Classless Struggle?', in E. Balibar and I. Wallerstein, *Race, Nation, Class: Ambiguous Identities* (C. Turner, tr.), London: Verso, 153–84.

Bauman, Z. 1982, *Memories of Class*, London: Routledge.

Bauman, Z. 1989, 'Hermeneutics and Modern Social Theory', in D. Held and J.B. Thompson (eds) *Social Theory of Modern Societies: Anthony Giddens and his Critics*, Cambridge: Cambridge University Press.

Beck, U. 1992, *Risk Society: Towards a New Modernity*, London: Sage.

Bell, D. 1974, *The Coming of Post-Industrial Society*, London: Heinemann.

Bendix, R. and S.M. Lipset, 1967, 'Karl Marx's Theory of Social Classes', in R. Bendix and S.M. Lipset (eds) *Class, Status and Power*, London: Routledge.

Bishop, Y.M.M., S.E. Fienberg, and P.W. Holland, 1975, *Discrete Multivariate Analysis: Theory and Practice*, Cambridge, Mass.: MIT Press.

Blau, P. and O.D. Duncan, 1967, *The American Occupational Structure*, New York: John Wiley.

Blossfeld, H.P. and Y. Shavit (eds), 1993, *Persisting Inequality: Changing Educational Stratification in Thirteen Countries*, Boulder: Westview Press.

Böröcz, J. 1989, 'Mapping the Class Structures of State Socialism in East-Central Europe', *Research in Social Stratification and Mobility*, 8: 279–309.

Bottomore, T. 1991, *Classes in Modern Society* (second edition), London: Harper Collins.

Bottomore, T. and R. Brym, 1989, *The Capitalist Class: An International Study*, Hemel Hempstead: Harvester Wheatsheaf.

Bourdieu, P. 1977, *Outline of a Theory of Practice*, Cambridge: Cambridge University Press.

Braverman, H. 1974, *Labour and Monopoly Capital*, New York: Basic Books.

Breen, R. 1987, 'Sources of Cross-National Variation in Mobility Regimes: English, French and Swedish data Reanalysed', *Sociology*, 22,1:75–90.

Breen, R. 1994, 'Measuring Inequality in Mobility Tables'. Unpublished manuscript.

Breen, R., D.F. Hannan, D.B. Rottman, and C.T. Whelan, 1990, *Understanding Contemporary Ireland: State, Class and Development in the Republic of Ireland*, London: Macmillan.

Breen, R. and C.T. Whelan, 1993, 'From Ascription to Achievement? Origins, Education and Entry to the Labour Force in the Republic of Ireland during the Twentieth Century', *Acta Sociologica*, 36, 1: 3–17.

Breen, R. and C.T. Whelan, 1994, 'Gender and Class Mobility: Evidence from the Republic of Ireland', *Sociology*, forthcoming.

Brewer, R. 1986, 'A Note on the Changing Status of the Registrar General's Classification of Occupations', *British Journal of Sociology*, 37, 2: 131–40.

Burawoy, M. 1985, *The Politics of Production: Factory Regimes Under Capitalism and Socialism*, London: Verso.

Burawoy, Michael and Pavel Krotov, 1992, 'The Soviet Transition from Socialism to Capitalism', *American Sociological Review*, 57, 1:1–15.

Burawoy, M. and J. Lukács, 1992, *The Radiant Past: Ideology and Reality in Hungary's Road to Capitalism*, Chicago: University of Chicago Press.

Carchedi, G. 1989, 'Classes and Class Analysis', 105–25, in E. Wright (ed.) *The Debate on Classes*, London: Verso.

Carling, A. 1991, *Social Division*, London: Verso.

Castles, F. 1988, *The State and Political Theory*, Princeton, NJ: Princeton University Press.

Chandler, A.D., Jr. 1984, 'The Emergence of Managerial Capitalism', *Business History Review*, 58, Winter: 473–503. Reprinted in M. Granovetter and R. Swedberg (eds) *The Sociology of Economic Life*, Boulder: Westview Press, 1992.

Chase-Dunn, C. 1989, *Global Formation: Structures of the World-Economy*, Oxford: Basil Blackwell.

Clark, T.N. and S.M. Lipset, 1991, 'Are Social Classes Dying?' *International Sociology*, 6, 4: 397–410.

Clark, J. C. Modgil and S. Modgil (eds), 1990, *John H. Goldthorpe: Consensus and Controversy*, London: Falmer Press.

Coleman, J.S. 1990, *Foundations of Social Theory*, Cambridge, Mass.: Harvard University Press.

Coleman, J.S. and T.J. Farraro, 1992, *Rational Choice, Advocacy and Critique*, Beverley Hills: Sage.

Collins, R. 1992, 'Weber's Last Theory of Capitalism: A Systematization', 85–109, in M. Granovetter and R. Swedberg (eds) *The Sociology of Economic Life*, Boulder: Westview Press, reprinted from *American Sociological Review* (1980), 45, 6: 925–42.

Crewe, I. 1986, 'On the Death and Resurrection of Class Voting: Some Comments on *How Britain Votes*', *Political Studies*, 34: 620–38.

Crompton, R. 1980, 'Class Mobility in Modern Britain', *Sociology*, 14, 1: 117–119.

Crompton, R. 1993, *Class and Stratification: An Introduction to Current Debates*, Cambridge: Polity Press.

Crompton R. and G. Jones, 1984, *White Collar Proletariat: Deskilling and Gender in Clerical Work*, London: Macmillan.

Dahrendorf, R. 1959, *Class and Class Conflict in Industrial Society*, London: Routledge.

Dale, A. 1986, 'Social Class and the Self-Employed', *Sociology*, 20, 30: 430–4.

Dale, A., G.N. Gilbert and S. Arber, 1985, 'Integrating Women into Class Theory', *Sociology*, 19, 3: 384–408.

Dex, S. 1990, 'Goldthorpe on Class and Gender: The Case Against', in J. Clarke, C. Modgil and S. Modgil (eds) *John H. Goldthorpe: Concensus and Controversy*, London: Falmer Press.

Drozdiak, William 1994, 'Revving Up Europe's "Four Motors"', *The Washington Post*, March 27, 1994, p. C3.

Duncan, O.D. 1966, 'Methodological Issues in the Analysis of Social Mobility', in N.J. Smelser and S.M. Lipset (eds) *Social Structure and Mobility in Economic Development*, New York: Aldine.

Dunleavy, P. and C.T. Husbands, 1985, *British Democracy at the Crossroads*, London: Allen and Unwin.

Earle, P. 1989, *The Making of the English Middle Class: Business, Society and Family Life in London 1660–1730*, London: Methuen.

Edgell, S. 1993, *Class*, London: Routledge.

Elias, N. 1978, *What is Sociology?*, London: Hutchinson.

Elster, J. 1982, 'Marxism, Functionalism and Game Theory: The Case for Methodological Individualism', *Theory and Society*, 11, July: 453–82.

Elster, J. 1989, *Nuts and Bolts for the Social Sciences*, Cambridge: Cambridge University Press.

Elster, J. (ed.) 1986, *Rational Choice*, Oxford: Basil Blackwell.

Erikson, R. 1984, 'Social Class of Men, Women and Families', *Sociology*, 18, 4: 500–14.

Erikson, R. and J.H. Goldthorpe, 1985, 'Are American Rates of Social Mobility Exceptionally High? New Evidence on an Old Issue', *European Sociological Review*, 1, 1: 1–22.

Erikson, R. and J.H. Goldthorpe, 1987a, 'Commonality and Variation in Social Fluidity in Industrial Nations, Part II: A Model for Evaluating the "FJH Hypothesis"', *European Sociological Review*, 3, 1: 54–77.

Erikson, R. and J.H. Goldthorpe, 1987b, 'Commonality and Variation in Social Fluidity in Industrial Nations, Part I: The Model of Core Social Fluidity Applied', *European Sociological Review*, 3, 2: 145–66.

Erikson, R. and J.H. Goldthorpe, 1992a, 'Individual or Family? Results from two Approaches to Class Assignment', *Acta Sociologica*, 35: 95–106.

Erikson R. and J.H. Goldthorpe, 1992b, *The Constant Flux: A Study of Class Mobility in Industrial Societies*, Oxford: Clarendon Press.

Erikson, R., J.H. Goldthorpe, and L. Portocarero, 1979, 'Intergenerational Class Mobility in Three Western European Societies: England, France and Sweden', *British Journal of Sociology*, 30, 4: 415–41.

Erikson, R., J.H. Goldthorpe, and L. Portocarero, 1982, 'Social Fluidity in Industrial Nations: England, France and Sweden', *British Journal of Sociology*, 33, 1: 1–34.

Erikson, R. and S. Pontinen, 1984, 'Social Mobility in Finland and Sweden: A Comparison of Men and Women', in R. Alapuro (ed.) *Small States in Comparative Perspective*, Oslo: Norwegian University Press.

Esping-Andersen, G. 1990, *The Three Worlds of Welfare Capitalism*, Princeton, NJ: Princeton University Press.

Esping-Andersen, G. 1993, 'Post-industrial Class Structures: An Analytical Framework', in G. Esping-Andersen (ed.) *Changing Classes: Stratification and Mobility in Post-Industrial Societies*, Newbury Park, California: Sage.

Evans, P. and T.D. Stephens, 1988, 'Development and the World Economy', in N. Smelser (ed.) *Handbook of Sociology*, London: Sage.

Featherman, D.L., F.L. Jones, and R.M. Hauser, 1975, 'Assumptions of Social Mobility Research in the US: The Case of Occupational Status', *Social Science Research*, 4: 329–60.

Fienberg, S.E. 1977, *The Analysis of Cross-Classified Categorical Data*, Cambridge, Mass.: MIT Press.

Frazier, E. Franklin 1957, *The Black Bourgeoisie*, New York: Macmillan.

Fukuyama, F. 1989, 'The End of History?', *The National Interest*, 16: 3–18.

Gallie, D. 1988, 'Employment, Unemployment and Social Structure' in D. Gallie (ed.) *Employment in Britain*, Oxford: Blackwell.

Ganzeboom, H., R. Luijkx, and D.J. Treiman, 1989, 'Intergenerational Class Mobility in Comparative Perspective', *Research in Social Stratification and Mobility*, 8: 3–55.

Garfinkel, H. 1967, *Studies in Ethnomethodology*, Englewood Cliffs, NJ: Prentice-Hall.

Giddens, A. 1971, *Capitalism and Modern Social Theory: An Analysis of the Writings of Marx, Durkheim and Max Weber*. Cambridge: Cambridge University Press.

Giddens, A. 1973, *The Class Structure of the Advanced Societies*, London: Hutchinson.

Giddens, A. 1980, *The Class Structure of the Advanced Societies*, (second edition), London: Hutchinson.

Giddens, A. 1982, 'Action, Structure and Power', in A. Giddens, *Profiles and Critiques in Social Theory*, London: Macmillan.

Giddens, A. 1984, *The Constitution of Society*, Cambridge: Polity Press.

Giddens, A. 1985, *The Nation-State and Violence*, Cambridge: Cambridge University Press.

Goldthorpe, J.H. 1980, 'Class Mobility in Modern Britain: A Reply to Crompton', *Sociology*, 14, 1: 121–3.

Goldthorpe, J.H. 1982, 'On the Service Class: its Formation and Future', in A. Giddens and G. Mackenzie (eds) *Social Class and the Division of Labour: Essays in Honour of Ilya Neustadt*, Cambridge: Cambridge University Press.

Goldthorpe, J.H. 1983, 'Women and Class Analysis: In Defence of the Conventional View', *Sociology*, 17, 4: 465–88.

Goldthorpe, J.H. 1984, 'Women and Class Analysis: A Reply to the Replies', *Sociology*, 18, 4: 491–500.

Goldthorpe, J.H. 1985, 'On Economic Development and Social Mobility', *British Journal of Sociology*, 36, 4: 549–73.

Goldthorpe, J.H. 1990, 'A Response', in J. Clark, C. Modgil, and S. Modgil (eds) *John H. Goldthorpe: Consensus and Controversy*, London: Falmer Press.

Goldthorpe, J.H. and C. Llewellyn, 1977, 'Class Mobility in Modern Britain: Three Theses Examined', *British Journal of Sociology*, 28, 2: 257–87.

Goldthorpe, J.H. with C. Llewellyn and C. Payne, 1980 (second edition 1987), *Social Mobility and Class Structure in Modern Britain*, Oxford: Clarendon Press.

Goldthorpe, J. H., D. Lockwood, F. Bechhoffer, and J. Platt, 1969, *The Affluent Worker in the Class Structure*, Cambridge: Cambridge University Press.

Goldthorpe, J.H. and G. Marshall, 1992, 'The Promising Future of Class Analysis: A Response to Recent Critiques', *Sociology*, 26, 3: 381–400.

Goldthorpe, J.H. and C. Payne, 1986, 'Trends in Intergenerational Mobility in England and Wales, 1979–83', *Sociology*, 20, 1: 1–24.

Goodman, Leo A. 1979, 'Simple Models for the Analysis of Association in Cross-classifications having Ordered Categories', *Journal of the American Statistical Society*, 65:225–56.

Grabb, E.G. 1984, *Social Inequality: Classical and Contemporary Theorists*, Toronto: Holt Rinehart and Winston.

Grimes, M.D. 1991, *Class in Twentieth-Century American Sociology: An Analysis of Theories and Measurement Strategies*, New York: Praeger.

Hakim, C. 1992, 'Explaining Trends in Occupational Segregation: The Measurement, Causes and Circumstances of the Sexual Division of Labour', *European Sociological Review*, 8, 2: 127–52.

Haller, M. 1990, 'European Class Structure: Does it Exist?', in M. Haller (ed.) *Class Structure in Europe: New Findings from East–West Comparisons of Social Structure and Mobility*, London: M.E. Sharpe.

Haller, M., T. Kolosi, and P. Robert, 1990, 'Social Mobility in Austria, Czechoslovakia, and Hungary: An Investigation of the Effects of

Industrialization, Socialist Revolution, and National Uniqueness', in M. Haller (ed.) *Class Structure in Europe: New Findings from East–West Comparisons of Social Structure and Mobility*, London: M.E. Sharpe.

Hamilton, M. and M. Hirszowicz, 1987, *Class and Inequality in Pre-industrial, Capitalist and Communist Countries*, Hemel Hempstead: Harvester Wheatsheaf.

Hamnett, C. 1989, 'Consumption and class in contemporary Britain', in C. Hamnett, L. McDowell and P. Sarre (eds) *Restructuring Britain: The Changing Social Structure*, London: Sage.

Harris, A.L. 1939, 'Pure Capitalism and the Disappearance of the Middle Class', *Journal of Political Economy*, 47, 3: 328–56.

Harvey, D. 1989, *The Condition of Postmodernity: An Enquiry into The Origins of Cultural Change*, Oxford: Basil Blackwell.

Hayes, B.C. and F.L. Jones, 1992, 'Marriage and Political Partisanship in Australia: Do Wives' Characteristics Make a Difference?', *Sociology*, 26, 1: 81–101.

Hayes, B.C. and R.L. Miller, 1993, 'The Silenced Voice: Female Social Mobility Patterns with Particular Reference to the British Isles', *British Journal of Sociology*, 44, 4: 653–72

Hazelrigg, L.E. 1974, 'Partitioning Structural Effects and Endogenous Mobility Processes in the Measurement of Vertical Occupational Status Change', *Acta Sociologica*, 17, 2: 115–39.

Heath, A.F. and N. Britten, 1984, 'Women's Jobs do Make a Difference', *Sociology*, 18, 4: 475–90.

Heath, A.F. and P. Clifford, 1990, 'Class Inequalities in the Twentieth Century', *Journal of the Royal Statistical Society, Series A*, 153, 1: 1–16.

Heath, A.F. and P. Clifford, 1993, 'The Political Consequences of Social Mobility', *Journal of the Royal Statistical Society, Series A*, 156, 1: 51–62.

Heath, A.F., R. Jowell, and J. Curtice, 1985, *How Britain Votes*, Oxford: Pergamon.

Heath, A.F., R. Jowell, and J. Curtice, 1987, 'Trendless Fluctuation: Relative Class Voting 1964–83' *Political Studies*, 35, 2: 256–77.

Heath, A.F., C. Mills, and J. Roberts, 1992, 'Towards Meritocracy? Recent Evidence on an Old Problem', in C. Crouch and A. Heath (eds) *Social Research and Social Reform*, Oxford: Clarendon Press.

Hechter, M. 1975, *Internal Colonialism: The Celtic Fringe in British National Development, 1536–1966*, London: Routledge and Kegan Paul.

Hechter, M. 1987, *Principles of Group Solidarity*, Berkeley: University of California Press.

Hexter, J.H. 1961, *Reappraisals in History*, London: Longmans.

Hindess, B. 1987, *Politics and Class Analysis*, Oxford: Blackwell.

Hobsbawm, E. 1981, 'The Forward March of Labour Halted', in M. Jacques and F. Mulhern (eds) *The Forward March of Labour Halted?*, London: New Left Books.

Holtmann, D. and H. Strasser, 1990, 'Comparing Class Structures and Class Consciousness in Western Societies', *International Journal of Sociology*, 19, 1: 1–27.

Holton, R.J. and B.S. Turner, 1989, 'Has Class Analysis a Future? Max Weber and the Challenge of Liberalism to Gemeinschaftlich Accounts of Class', in R.J. Holton and B.S. Turner (eds) *Max Weber on Economy and Society*, London: Routledge.

Hope, K. 1981, 'Vertical mobility in Britain: A Structured Analysis', *Sociology*, 15, 1: 19–55.

Hope, K. 1982, 'Vertical and Non-vertical Class Mobility in Three Countries', *American Sociological Review*, 47, 1: 99–113.

Hout, M., C. Brooks and J. Manza, 1993, 'The Persistence of Classes in Postindustrial Societies' *International Sociology*, 8 (September) : 259–68.

Hutchinson, B. 1958, 'Structural and Exchange Mobility in the Assimilation of Immigrants to Brazil', *Population Studies*, 12: 111–20.

Jencks, Christopher 1993, *Rethinking Social Policy: Race, Poverty and the Underclass*, New York: Harper Perennial (first published 1992).

Kamolnick, P. 1988, *Classes: A Marxist Critique*, Dix Halls, NY: General Hall.

Katz, M.B. 1993, 'The Urban "Underclass" as a Metaphor of Social Transformation', in M. Katz (ed.) *The 'Underclass' Debate: Views From History*, Princeton, NJ: Princeton University Press.

Kerr,C. 1969, *Marshall, Marx and Modern Times*, Cambridge: Cambridge University Press.

Kerr, C., J.T. Dunlop, F. Harbison, and C.A. Myers, 1960, *Industrialism and Industrial Man: The Problems of Labour and the Management of Economic Growth*, Cambridge, Mass.: Harvard University Press.

Leete, R and J. Fox, 1977, 'Registrar General's Social Classes', *Population Trends*, 8: 1–17.

Lenski, G. 1966, *Power and Privilege: A Theory of Social Stratification*, New York: McGraw-Hill.

Lenski, G. 1978, 'Marxist Experiments in Destratification: An Appraisal', *Social Forces*, 57, 2: 364–83.

Linder, M. and J. Houghton, 1990, 'Self-Employment and the Petty Bourgeoisie: Comment on Steinmetz and Wright', *American Journal of Sociology*, 96, 3: 727–35.

Lockwood, D. 1958, *The Blackcoated Worker*, London: Allen and Unwin.

Lockwood, D. 1981, 'The Weakest Link in the Chain? Some Comments on the Marxist Theory of Action', *Research in the Sociology of Work*, 1: 435–81.

Lukes, S. 1984, The Future of British Socialism?', in B. Pimlott (ed.) *Fabian Essays in Socialist Thought*, London: Heinemann.

Machina, M. 1987, 'Choice Under Uncertainty: Problems Solved and Unsolved', *Journal of Economic Perspectives*, 1: 121–54.

Maddison, A. 1982, *Phases of Capitalist Development*, Oxford: Oxford University Press.

Marsh, C. 1986, 'Social Class and Occupation', in R. Burgess (ed.) *Key Variables in Social Investigation*, London: Routledge and Kegan Paul.

Marshall, G. 1987, 'What is Happening to the Working Class?', *Social Studies Review*, 2, 3: 37–40.

Marshall, G. 1990, *In Praise of Sociology*, London: Unwin Hyman.

Marshall, G. 1991, 'In Defence of Class Analysis: A Comment on R.E. Pahl', *International Journal of Urban and Regional Research*, 15, 1: 114–18.

Marshall, G., H. Newby, D. Rose and C. Vogler, 1988, *Social Class in Modern Britain*, London: Unwin Hyman.

Marshall, G., S. Roberts, C. Burgoyne, A. Swift, and D. Routh, 1994, 'Class, Gender and the Asymmetry Hypothesis'. Unpublished manuscript.

Martin, R. and J. Wallace, 1984, *Working Women in Recession*, Oxford: Oxford University Press.

Marx, Karl and Friedrich Engels, 1848/1977, *The Communist Manifesto*, in D. McLellan (ed.) *Karl Marx: Selected Writings*, Oxford: Oxford University Press, 221–46.

Marx, Karl and Friedrich Engels, 1965, *The German Ideology*, London: Lawrence and Wishart.

Matras, J. 1975, *Social Inequality, Stratification, and Mobility*, Englewood Cliffs, NJ: Prentice-Hall.

McClendon, M.J. 1977, 'Structural and Exchange Components of Vertical Mobility', *American Sociological Review*, 42, 1: 56–74.

McClendon, M.J. 1980, 'Structural and Exchange Components of Occupational Mobility: A Cross-National Analysis', *The Sociological Quarterly*, 21: 493–509.

McNall, S., G. Rhoda. F. Levine, and R. Fantasia (eds), 1991, *Bringing Class Back In: Contemporary and Historical Perspectives,* Boulder: Westview.

McRae, S. 1990, 'Women and Class Analysis', in J. Clarke, C. Modgill and S. Modgill (eds) *John H. Goldthorpe: Consensus and Controversy*, London: Falmer Press.

Merton, R. 1993 (first edition 1965), *On the Shoulders of Giants: A Shandean Postscript 'The Post-Italianate Edition'*, Chicago: University of Chicago Press.

Miller, S.M. 1960, 'Comparative Social Mobility', *Current Sociology*, 9: 1–89.

Mills, C. Wright 1962, *The Marxists*, Harmondsworth: Penguin.

Mouzelis, N.P. 1986, *Politics in the Semi-Periphery*, London: Macmillan.

Murgatroyd, L. 1984, 'Women, Men and the Social Grading of Occupations', *British Journal of Sociology*, 35, 4: 473–97.

Myles, J. 1988, 'Postwar Capitalism and the Extension of Social Security into a Retirement Age' in M. Weir, A. Orloff and T. Skocpol (eds) *The Politics of Social Security in the United States*, Princeton: Princeton University Press.

Newby, H., C. Vogler, D. Rose, and G. Marshall, 1985, 'From Class Structure to Class Action: British Working-Class Politics in the 1980s', in B. Roberts, R. Finnegan, and D. Gallie (eds) *New Approaches to Economic Life*, Manchester: Manchester University Press.

Nisbet, R. 1959, 'The Decline and Fall of Social Class', *Pacific Sociological Review*, 2: 11–17.

Offe, C. 1985, 'Work: the Key Sociological Category?', in C. Offe, *Disorganised Capitalism*, Cambridge: Polity Press.

Omi, Michael and Howard Winant, 1994, *Racial Formation in the United States from the 1960s to the 1990s*, New York: Routledge.

Outhwaite, W. 1987, *New Philosophies of Social Science: Realism, Hermeneutics and Critical Theory*, London: Macmillan.

Pahl, R.E. 1989, 'Is the Emperor Naked? Some Questions on the Adequacy of Sociological Theory in Urban and Regional Research', *International Journal of Urban and Regional Research*, 13, 4: 709–20.

Parkin, F. 1971, *Class Inequality and Political Order: Social Stratification in Capitalist and Communist Societies*, London: McGibbon and Kee.

Parkin, F. 1979, *Marxism and Class Theory: A Bourgeois Critique*, New York: Columbia University Press.

Parsons, T. 1960, *Structure and Process in Modern Society*, Glencoe, Ill.: Free Press.

Parsons, T. 1964, 'Evolutionary Universals in Society', *American Sociological Review*, 29: 339–57.

Parsons, T. 1970, 'Equality and Inequality in Modern Society, or Social Stratification Revisited', in E.O. Laumann (ed.) *Social Stratification: Research and Theory for the 1970s*, New York: Bobs-Merrill, 13–72.

Pawson, R. 1989, *A Measure for Measures: A Manifesto for Empirical Sociology*, London: Routledge.

Polanyi, K. 1944, *The Great Transformation*, New York: Farrar & Rinehart.

Poulantzas, N. 1975, *Classes in Contemporary Capitalism*, London: New Left Books.

Poulantzas, N. 1977, 'The New Petty Bourgeoisie', in A. Hunt (ed.) *Class and Class Structure*, London: Lawrence and Wishart.

Przeworski, A. 1991, *Democracy and the Market: Political and Economic Reforms in Eastern Europe and Latin America*, Cambridge: Cambridge University Press.

Przeworski, A., R.R. Barnett, and E. Underhill, 1980, 'The Evolution of the Class Structure of France, 1901–1968', *Economic Development and Cultural Change*, 28, July: 725–52.

Przeworski, A. and J. Sprague, 1986, *Paper Stones: A History of Electoral Socialism*, Chicago: University of Chicago Press.

Psacharapoulos, G. 1977, 'Family Background, Education and Achievement: A Path Model of Earnings Determinants in the UK and Some Alternatives', *British Journal of Sociology*, 28, 3: 321–35.

Ragin, C. and J. Delacroix, 1979, 'Comparative Advantage, the World Division of Labour, and Underdevelopment', *Comparative Social Research*, 2: 181–214.

Reid, I. 1989, *Social Class Differences in Britain* (third edition), London: Fontana.

Remnick, David 1994, *Lenin's Tomb: The Last Days of the Soviet Empire*, New York: Vintage.

Roemer, J. 1982a, 'Analytical Foundations of Marxian Economic Theory', *Theory and Society*, 11: 513–20.

Roemer, J. 1982b, *A General Theory of Exploitation and Class*, Cambridge, Mass.: Harvard University Press.

Rose, R. 1985, 'The Significance of Public Employment', in R. Rose (ed.) *Public Employment in Western Nations*, Cambridge: Cambridge University Press.

Runciman, W.G. 1990, 'How Many Classes are there in Contemporary British Society?', *Sociology*, 24, 3: 377–96.

Sarvlik, B. and I. Crewe, 1983, *Decade of Dealignment: The Conservative Victory of 1979 and Electoral Trends in the 1970s*, Cambridge: Cambridge University Press.

Saunders, P. 1981, 'Beyond Housing Classes: The Sociological Significance of Private Property Rights in Means of Consumption', *International Journal of Urban and Regional Research*, 8: 202–27.

Saunders, P. 1990, *A Nation of Home Owners*, London: Unwin Hyman.

Scase, R. 1992, *Class*, Buckingham: Open University Press.

Scase, R. and R. Goffee, 1982, *The Entrepreneurial Middle Class*, London: Croom Helm.

Scott, J. 1985, *Corporations, Classes and Capitalism*, London: Hutchinson.

Sewell, W.H. and R.M. Hauser, 1975, *Occupation and Earnings: Achievement in the Early Career*, New York: Academic Press.

Snyder, D. and E. Kick, 1979, 'Structural Position in the World System and Economic Growth 1955–70: A Multiple Network Analysis in Transnational Interactions', *American Journal of Sociology*, 84, 5: 1096–126.

Sobel, M.E. 1983, 'Structural Mobility, Circulation Mobility and the Analysis of Occupational Mobility: A Conceptual Mismatch', *American Sociological Review*, 48, 6: 721–7.

Sobel, M.E., M. Hout, and O.D. Duncan, 1985, 'Exchange, Structure and Symmetry in Occupational Mobility', *American Journal of Sociology*, 91, 2: 359–72.

Sombart, W. 1907/76, *Why is there no Socialism in the United States?*, London: Macmillan.

Somers, M.R. 1993, 'Citizenship and the Place of the Public Sphere: Law, Community, and Political Culture in the Transition to Democracy', *American Sociological Review*, 58, 5: 587–620.

Sorenson, A.B. 1986, 'Theory and Methodology in Social Stratification', in U. Himmelstrand (ed.) *Sociology; From Crisis to Science*, London: Sage.

Sorenson, A.B. 1991, 'On the Usefulness of Class Analysis in Research on Social Mobility and Socioeconomic Inequality', *Acta Sociologica*, 34: 71–87.

Stanfield, J.H. 1991, 'Racism in American and in Other Race-centered Nation-states: Synchronic Considerations', *International Journal of Comparative Sociology*, 32: 243–60.

Stanworth, M. 1984, 'Women and Class Analysis: A Reply to John Goldthorpe', *Sociology*, 18, 2: 159–70.

Steinberg, Stephen 1989, *The Ethnic Myth: Race, Ethnicity and Class in America: Updated and Expanded Edition*, Boston, Mass.: Beacon Press.

Steinmetz, G. and E.O. Wright, 1989, 'The Fall and Rise of the Petty Bourgeoisie: Changing Patterns of Self-Employment in the Postwar United States', *American Journal of Sociology*, 94, 5: 973–1018.

Steinmetz, G. and E.O. Wright, 1990, 'Reply to Linder and Houghton', *American Journal of Sociology*, 96, 3: 736–40.

Sugrue, T.J. 1993, 'The Structures of Urban Poverty: The Reorganization of Space and Work in Three Periods of American History', in M. Katz (ed.) *The 'Underclass' Debate: Views From History*, Princeton NJ: Princeton University Press.

Swedberg, R. 1990, *Economics and Sociology*, Princeton, NJ: Princeton University Press.

Szymanski, A. 1983, *Class Structure: A Critical Perspective*, New York: Praeger.

Teckenberg, W. 1990, 'The Stability of Occupational Structures, Social Mobility and Interest Formation: The USSR as an Estatist Society in Comparison with Class Societies', pp.24–60 in M. Haller (ed.) *Class Structure in Europe: East–West Comparisons of Social Structure and Mobility*, London: M.E. Sharpe.

Thomas, M.E. 1993, 'Race, Class, and Personal Income: An Empirical Test of the Declining Significance of Race Thesis, 1968–1988', *Social Problems*, 40, August: 328–42.

Thompson, E.P. 1968 (first edition 1963), *The Making of the English Working Class*, Harmondsworth: Pelican.

Treiman, D.J. 1970, 'Industrialization and Social Stratification', in E.O. Laumann (ed.) *Social Stratification: Research and Theory for the 1970s*, New York: Bobs-Merrill.

Van Dijk, T.A. 1987, *Communicating Racism: Ethnic Prejudice in Thought and Talk*, Newbury Park, Calif.: Sage.

Van Parijs, P. 1989, 'A Revolution in Class Theory', in E.O. Wright (ed.) *The Debate on Classes*, London: Verso.

Vogler, Carolyn M. 1985, *The Nation State: The Neglected Dimension of Class*, Aldershot: Gower.

Walby, S. 1986, 'Gender, Class and Stratification: Towards a New Approach' in R. Crompton and M. Mann (eds) *Gender and Stratification*, Oxford: Basil Blackwell.

Wallerstein, I. 1974, *The Modern World System: Capitalist Agriculture and the Origins of the European World Economy in the Sixteenth Century*, New York: Academic Press.

Wallerstein, I. 1980, *The Modern World System II: Mercantalism and the Consolidation of the European World Economy*, New York: Academic Press.

Wallerstein, I. 1991, 'Class Conflict in the Capitalist World-Economy', in E. Balibar and I. Wallerstein, *Race, Nation, Class: Ambiguous Identities* (C. Turner, tr.), London: Verso: 115–24.

Waters, M. 1991, 'Collapse and Convergence in Class Theory', *Theory and Society*, 20: 141–72.

Weber, M. 1949, *The Methodology of the Social Sciences*, Glencoe, Ill.: Free Press.

Weber, M. 1961 (first edition 1923), *General Economic History*, New York: Collier Books.

Weber, M. 1968 (first edition 1923), *Economy and Society: An Outline of Interpretive Sociology*, New York: Bedminster Press.

Weede, E. and J. Kummer, 1985, 'Some Criticisms of Recent Work on World System Status, Inequality, and Democracy', *International Journal of Comparative Sociology*, 26, 3–4: 132–48.

Westergaard, J.H. 1970, 'The Rediscovery of the Cash Nexus', in R. Miliband and J. Saville (eds) *The Socialist Register, 1970*, London: Merlin Press.

Wilson, W.J. 1978, *The Declining Significance of Race: Blacks and Changing American Institutions*, Chicago: University of Chicago Press.

Wilson, W.J. 1987, *The Truly Disadvantaged: The Inner City, The Underclass, and Public Policy*, Chicago: University of Chicago Press.

Wilson W.J. 1991, 'Studying Inner-City Dislocations: The Challenge of Public Agenda Research', *American Sociological Review*, 56, 1, February: 1–14.

Worsley, P. (ed.) 1977, *Introducing Sociology* (second edition), Harmondsworth: Penguin.

Wright, E.O. 1976, 'Class Boundaries in Advanced Capitalist Societies', *New Left Review*, 98, July/August: 3–41.

Wright, E.O. 1978, *Class, Crisis and the State*, London: New Left Books.

Wright, E.O. 1985, *Classes*, London: Verso.

Wright, E.O. 1989a, 'A General Framework for the Analysis of Class Structure', in E.O. Wright (ed.) *The Debate on Classes*, London: Verso.

Wright, E.O. 1989b, 'Rethinking, Once Again, the Concept of Class Structure', in E.O. Wright (ed.) *The Debate on Classes*, London: Verso.

Wright, E.O., C. Costello, D. Hachen, and J. Sprague, 1982, 'The American Class Structure', *American Sociological Review*, 47, 6: 709–26.

Wright, E.O. and B. Martin, 1987, 'The Transformation of the American Class Structure', *American Journal of Sociology*, 93, 1: 1–29.

Wright, E.O. and L. Perrone, 1977, 'Marxist Class Categories and Income Inequality', *American Sociological Review*, 42, 1: 32–55.

Wright, E.O. and K.Y. Shin, 1988, 'Temporality and Class Analysis: A Comparative Study of the Effects of Class Trajectory and Class Structure in Sweden and the United States', *Sociological Theory*, 6 Spring: 58–84.

Young, M. and P. Willmott, 1957, *Family and Kinship in East London*, London: Routledge and Kegan Paul.

INDEX